THE BEDFORD SERIES IN HISTORY AND CULTURE

Voices of Decolonization

A Brief History with Documents

Related Titles in
THE BEDFORD SERIES IN HISTORY AND CULTURE
Advisory Editors: Lynn Hunt, *University of California, Los Angeles*
David W. Blight, *Yale University*
Bonnie G. Smith, *Rutgers University*
Natalie Zemon Davis, *University of Toronto*

Voices of Decolonization

A Brief History with Documents

Todd Shepard

Johns Hopkins University

BEDFORD / ST. MARTIN'S   Boston ◆ New York

For Bedford / St. Martin's

Publisher for History: Mary V. Dougherty
Senior Executive Editor for History: William J. Lombardo
Director of Development for History: Jane Knetzger
Publishing Services Manager: Andrea Cava
Production Supervisor: Victoria Anzalone
Executive Marketing Manager: Sandra McGuire
Editorial Assistant: Laura Kintz
Project Management: Books By Design, Inc.
Cartography: Mapping Specialists, Ltd.
Text Design: Claire Seng-Niemoeller
Cover Design: Marine Miller
Cover Photo: Opera Square, Cairo, January 9, 1954. Photographer: A. Masraff.
   Courtesy Getty Images.
Composition: Achorn International, Inc.
Printing and Binding: RR Donnelley and Sons

Manufactured in the United States of America.

9   8   7   6   5   4
f   e   d   c   b   a

For information, write: Bedford / St. Martin's, 75 Arlington Street, Boston, MA 02116
   (617-399-4000)

ISBN 978-1-4576-1815-4

Acknowledgments

Acknowledgments and copyrights are continued at the back of the book on page 178, which constitutes an extension of the copyright page. It is a violation of the law to reproduce these selections by any means whatsoever without the written permission of the copyright holder.

About the cover: Crowds protest British involvement in the Suez crisis in Cairo's Opera Square, January 9, 1954.

Foreword

The Bedford Series in History and Culture is designed so that readers can study the past as historians do.

The historian's first task is finding the evidence. Documents, letters, memoirs, interviews, pictures, movies, novels, or poems can provide facts and clues. Then the historian questions and compares the sources. There is more to do than in a courtroom, for hearsay evidence is welcome, and the historian is usually looking for answers beyond act and motive. Different views of an event may be as important as a single verdict. How a story is told may yield as much information as what it says.

Along the way the historian seeks help from other historians and perhaps from specialists in other disciplines. Finally, it is time to write, to decide on an interpretation and how to arrange the evidence for readers.

Each book in this series contains an important historical document or group of documents, each document a witness from the past and open to interpretation in different ways. The documents are combined with some element of historical narrative — an introduction or a biographical essay, for example — that provides students with an analysis of the primary source material and important background information about the world in which it was produced.

Each book in the series focuses on a specific topic within a specific historical period. Each provides a basis for lively thought and discussion about several aspects of the topic and the historian's role. Each is short enough (and inexpensive enough) to be a reasonable one-week assignment in a college course. Whether as classroom or personal reading, each book in the series provides firsthand experience of the challenge — and fun — of discovering, recreating, and interpreting the past.

Lynn Hunt
David W. Blight
Bonnie G. Smith
Natalie Zemon Davis

To Bonnie G. Smith

Preface

From 1945 to the early 1960s, decolonization—a "ring of fire burning all along the Tropics," according to the Senegalese historian Abdoulaye Ly—changed the lives of people across the globe. *Voices of Decolonization* is a sourcebook and history that allows students to understand this phenomenon's breadth across boundaries and its effects on both the colonizers and the colonized. It thereby enables readers to understand the course of decolonization as well as its legacy today. Rather than repeating established orthodoxies, the book offers opportunities for discussion and assessment from a variety of viewpoints. Giving voice to a wide range of experiences and analyses, it draws on the current explosion of scholarship and debate around decolonization in ways that enable students to reflect on the possibilities, limits, and meaning of the topic for themselves.

Part one offers a chronological narrative of key events and players that reveals, through both arguments between competing forces and acts of individual sacrifice, how movements and events around the world came together to become the phenomenon known as decolonization. The introduction focuses on the period from around 1945 to 1965 and shows how decolonization repeatedly intersected with three of the twentieth century's most important issues: (1) the cold war, (2) the tensions between the development of international institutions and pressing arguments for national self-determination, and (3) what W. E. B. DuBois termed the "color line." The introduction also examines how decolonization crossed boundaries, changing how individuals thought and states acted, and how it has continued to inspire people and debates from the late 1960s until today, thus illuminating how the "era of decolonization" became the "promise of decolonization." Most important, the introduction makes clear how the witnesses and actors featured in the documents in part two fit into this evolution.

The documents were selected to illustrate the intensity of worldwide debate about decolonization. As they clearly show, the reasons for decolonization, and the expectations of what would result from it, were multiple and often contradictory. The voices of the individuals introduced in part two—some famous, others unknown—reveal how much people cared about the struggle and how much they sacrificed for it. This part is organized to encourage discussions about decolonization that go beyond simple assessments of "success" or "failure," "good" or "bad." It highlights both people who defended the positive results of empire and those who yearned for liberation.

The five sections offer both a clear chronology and a sharp focus on distinct phases of decolonization, showing how this phenomenon transformed a *possibility* of freedom into a *promise*. Each section contains documents that not only relate to one another but also have clear connections to documents in other sections. This structure makes explicit the nature of contemporary conflicts between both ideas and armed forces, and it contributes to an understanding of how change happens.

The documents lend themselves to either in-class or assigned readings and also to discussion or writing assignments. They include not only diplomatic reports, political speeches, and descriptions of economic assessments, but also discussions of poetry and songs. Included are some of the most widely known written sources of the era (such as the UN Charter [1945] and the final declaration of the Bandung Conference [1955]) and some of the most famous voices (among them Ghana's Kwame Nkrumah, Trinidad and Tobago's Eric Williams, Britain's Winston Churchill, and the United States's Richard Wright). Yet also included are several little-known actors, such as a group of Vietnamese Roman Catholic bishops who lobbied for their country's independence, members of Kenya's Land and Free Army who wrote songs to promote their message, and a young South African woman who used poetry as a means of expressing her outrage over the violence in her country.

To facilitate student engagement with this history, introductory headnotes situate each document in its specific chronological and geographic context and indicate how the document speaks to larger questions. Footnotes clarify uncertainties about lesser-known names and the implications of sometimes complicated references. A chronology places decolonization in a wider historical context, questions for consideration link to specific documents, and a bibliography provides suggestions for further reading.

ACKNOWLEDGMENTS

I began this book after discussions with Bonnie G. Smith, moments in a long and ongoing conversation that shapes all the work I do. I dedicate this book to her.

A special thanks to everyone at Bedford/St. Martin's whose efforts made this book possible, especially Mary V. Dougherty, Traci M. Crowell, Elizabeth M. Welch, Heidi Hood, Laura Kintz, Andrea Cava, Nancy Benjamin, Eve Lehmann, and Barbara Jatkola.

Thanks also to the reviewers whose input helped make the manuscript better, especially Jeffrey Auerbach, California State University, Northridge; James Brennan, University of Illinois; James DeLorenzi, John Jay College; Edward Dickinson, University of California, Northridge; Christina Firpo, California Polytechnic State University, San Luis Obispo; and Kwaku Nti, Armstrong Atlantic State University.

The work of many scholars informed my choices and my arguments; some deserve special mention because of the direct assistance they offered: Jeffrey Ahlman, Carole Boyce Davies, Yonay Israel, Charles Keith, Christopher Lee, Muoki Mbunga, Cristiana Pugliese, Shira Robinson, Dr. Luis B. Serapião, Sarah A. Stein, Luise White, and my colleagues Beth Bailey, Sara Berry, Pier Larson, and Gabriel Paquette. Saïd Gahia's support made this project, and so much more, possible.

Todd Shepard

Contents

APPENDIXES

Maps

Maps

PART ONE

Introduction: Decolonization, from Unimaginable to Inevitable

In mid-August 1947, a ceremony took place at the House of Parliament in New Delhi, India. It began at 10:45 p.m. on the fourteenth in the Central Hall with a series of official speeches that culminated as the clock struck midnight—unexpectedly accompanied, an American witness recounted, by the blast of a conch-shell trumpet. Then attendees went into the night to join well-mannered revelers who had been allowed onto the grounds, as impromptu fireworks and more rambunctious celebrations spread throughout the surrounding metropolis and across the land. On July 5, 1962, a similar ceremony occurred in Algiers, the capital of Algeria. There, the celebrants marched through the seaside city in the late-morning sun as throngs hailed their passage, before taking to a public stage in the central plaza to watch a military parade. As in New Delhi fifteen years previously, the Algerian leaders who read the proclamations had fought long and hard to see this day arrive. What they announced was the end of many decades of European rule over their country; what people celebrated was national independence.

Between 1945 and 1965, proclamations that marked the end of direct foreign control and the establishment of independent states occurred over fifty times around the world, in capital cities ranging from Jakarta, Indonesia, to Accra, Ghana, and Kingston, Jamaica. Each was the result of wide-ranging developments that had absorbed many people locally but also had global echoes. In some places, the transfer of power happened

1

by mutual agreement between the colonial power and local leaders. In a few others, local politicians and elites had to be convinced to accept independence or simply had it thrust upon them. In many places, mass mobilization by people in the territory (on rare occasions supported by protests within the colonial power itself) forced the hand of colonial rulers. Often the end of foreign rule involved violence, sometimes at shocking levels. What particularly shocked observers was the scope—notably the number of local people killed by forces defending the status quo, and in kind, with the use of such spectacular forms of brutality as the beheading, castration, or evisceration of prisoners, the systematic use of torture and sexual assault, and the indiscriminate use of devastating weapons, including chemical weapons, in civilian areas. Perhaps the most remarkable thing is how these many different histories all came to seem part of one larger phenomenon. As an event, this "tide of History," as some writers began to describe it, inspired deep concern among world leaders and, even more, rising expectations among people across the globe. This was the era of the "end of empires," the "transfer of power," the "victories of liberation," "Europe's retreat from the world," and the "triumph of the third world," to identify some of the ways various commentators have described the events of those years. It was the culmination of decades of struggles and became a reference point for events and arguments that continue even today.

Let us focus for a moment on the ceremonies in New Delhi and Algiers, so as to gain some understanding of how this era developed, of how one thing led to other things, which is to say, of how these events and the people who created them changed history. In August 1947, it was Jawaharlal Nehru—the man who led the Indian National Congress of India and one of the most prominent leaders of the movement to free India from British rule—who dominated the stage. Strikingly absent from the proceedings was the most well-known Indian leader, Mohandas K. "Mahatma" Gandhi. This bespectacled and often barefooted man had catalyzed mass protests, popularized the embrace of nonviolent civil disobedience, and come to personify the insistent rejection of British efforts to delay independence. He chose to spend independence day in the sprawling coastal city then called Calcutta (now Kolkata), among poverty-stricken Muslims. This was just one sign of his dissatisfaction with how independence was to occur. In attendance, however, was Lord Mountbatten, the British aristocrat who, as the last viceroy of India, oversaw the end of British rule on the Indian subcontinent. He did so on the basis of a law passed earlier in 1947 by the British Parliament, which mandated a quick withdrawal. One decision the viceroy made, with the claim that ongoing conflict between Indian Muslims and Hindus rendered it necessary, was that on August 15, 1947, two states would be born as British India disappeared (see Map 1). This division, which separated large majority-Muslim areas in the west and east from the rest of India, was the reason Gandhi avoided the ceremonies. Before appearing in New Delhi on the evening of the fourteenth, Mountbatten spent the morning more than a thousand miles to the west, in Karachi. There, leaders of the All-India Muslim League, a group that had for years contested the "united India" approach of the Congress party, proclaimed the independence of the other state, the Dominion of Pakistan (later known as the Islamic Republic of Pakistan).

It was Nehru's midnight speech, however, that captured the world's imagination: "Long years ago we made a tryst with destiny, and now the time comes when we shall redeem our pledge, not wholly or in full measure, but very substantially," he began. "At the stroke of the midnight hour, when the world sleeps, India will awake to life and freedom. A moment comes, which comes but rarely in history, when we step out from the old to the new, when an age ends, and when the soul of a nation, long suppressed, finds utterance."[1] As an international audience listened, India's prime-minister-in-waiting gave voice to both stirring expectations for the future and long-standing hopes finally realized.

In Algiers, many of the men who marched triumphantly through the streets in July 1962 had not seen their homeland for years (see Map 2). The organization they helped lead, the National Liberation Front, known by its initials in French as the FLN, had waged violent war against French rule since 1954, and these leaders had been based abroad or held in French prisons. Victory had come when, in early 1962, the French consented to hold separate referendums in France and in Algeria to approve an agreement both sides had signed on to. On July 2, French authorities announced their recognition of Algerian independence, one day after the overwhelming yes vote in Algeria. FLN leaders, however, wanted to make it clear that it was they, not the colonizers, who had declared independence. After an internal discussion about the problematic symbolism of July 4, they decided to proclaim the establishment of an independent Algeria on July 5, 1962. The date was not just different from the birthday of the United States; it also marked the 132nd anniversary of the 1830 treaty that had ceded sovereignty of Algiers to the king of France, whose forces had invaded the region. France's most important colony, Algeria, unlike India, the "crown jewel of the British Empire," became independent as one country. Still, independence there sparked vigorous divisions among those who had fought for it. Some members

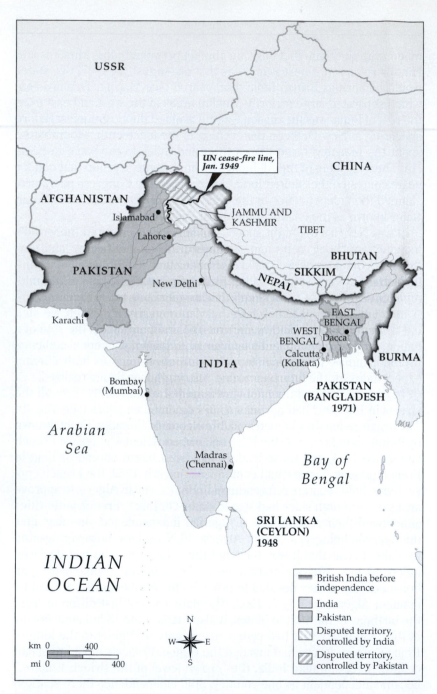

Map 1. *Partition of India, 1947*

4

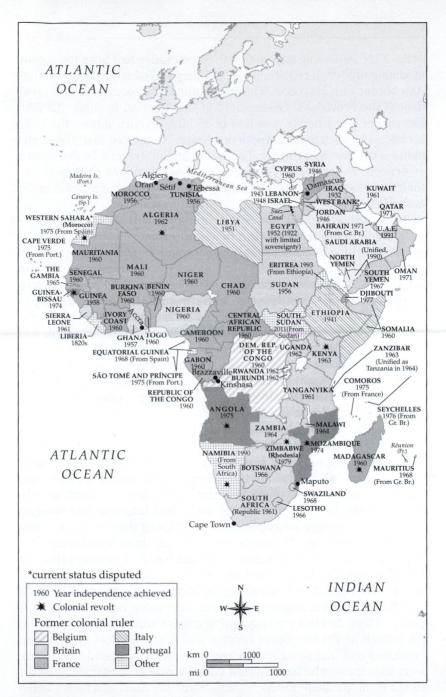

ATLANTIC
OCEAN

Madeira Is.
(Port.)

Canary Is.
(Sp.)

Algiers
Oran • Sétif • Tébessa

Mediterranean Sea

MOROCCO
1956

TUNISIA
1956

WESTERN SAHARA*
(Morocco)
1975 (From Spain)

CAPE VERDE
1975
(From Port.)

ALGERIA
1962

LIBYA
1951

Suez
Canal

CYPRUS
1960

SYRIA
1946

Damascus

1943 LEBANON
1948 ISRAEL

IRAQ
1932

KUWAIT
1961

WEST BANK*

JORDAN
1946

QATAR
1971

EGYPT
1952 (1922
with limited
sovereignty)

BAHRAIN 1971
(From Gr. Br.)

U.A.E.
1991

SAUDI ARABIA
(Unified,
1990)

NORTH
YEMEN

SOUTH
YEMEN
1967

OMAN
1971

MAURITANIA
1960

THE
GAMBIA
1965

SENEGAL
1960

MALI
1960

NIGER
1960

CHAD
1960

SUDAN
1956

ERITREA 1993
(From Ethiopia)

GUINEA-
BISSAU
1974

GUINEA
1958

BURKINA
FASO
1960

BENIN
1960

DJIBOUTI
1977

SIERRA
LEONE
1961

IVORY
COAST
1960

NIGERIA
1960

CENTRAL
AFRICAN
REPUBLIC
1960

SOUTH
SUDAN
2011(From
Sudan)

ETHIOPIA
1941

Accra

LIBERIA
1820s

GHANA
1957

TOGO
1960

CAMEROON
1960

SOMALIA
1960

EQUATORIAL GUINEA
1968 (From Spain)

GABON
1960

DEM. REP.
OF THE
CONGO
1960

UGANDA
1962

KENYA
1963

ZANZIBAR
1963
(Unified as
Tanzania in 1964)

SÃO TOMÉ AND PRÍNCIPE
1975 (From Port.)

Brazzaville
Kinshasa

RWANDA 1962
BURUNDI 1962

TANGANYIKA
1961

COMOROS
1975
(From France)

REPUBLIC OF
THE CONGO
1960

ANGOLA
1975

SEYCHELLES
1976 (From
Gr. Br.)

ATLANTIC
OCEAN

ZAMBIA
1964

MALAWI
1964

NAMIBIA 1990
(From
South
Africa)

ZIMBABWE
(Rhodesia)
1979

MOZAMBIQUE
1974

Réunion
(Fr.)

BOTSWANA
1966

MADAGASCAR
1960

MAURITIUS
1968
(From Gr. Br.)

Maputo

SOUTH
AFRICA
(Republic 1961)

SWAZILAND
1968

LESOTHO
1966

Cape Town •

*current status disputed

1960 Year independence achieved
✳ Colonial revolt

Former colonial ruler

Belgium   Italy
Britain   Portugal
France   Other

N
W   E
S

INDIAN
OCEAN

km 0   1000
mi 0   1000

Map 2. *New States of Africa and the Middle East, 1945–2011*

5

of the FLN leadership argued that their comrades had been too accommodating of French requirements, and they stayed with troops on Algeria's border with Morocco. With this in mind, the recently named president of the Provisional Government of the Algerian Republic (GPRA), Benyoucef Ben Khedda, was less poetic than Nehru during the radio broadcast he used to declare independence. He warned that "those who menace the necessary national cohesion and unity must be denounced or brought to see reason," and he called on his fellow citizens to end their festivities: "Tomorrow all national activity must begin again under normal conditions."[2]

These two celebrations of independence—New Delhi, August 15, 1947; Algiers, July 5, 1962—had much in common. Both had been eagerly anticipated by political organizations and individuals who ardently rejected European claims that ultimate decisions about how to govern their country were best made in London or Paris. Those who won independence presented themselves as the heirs to a long history of struggle. The Indian National Congress celebrated its status as the oldest political movement established in a colony by colonized people and dedicated to challenging the exercise of colonial power. The FLN raised the flag first waved by Emir Abd-al-Qadir a few years after the French invasion of 1830, as he rallied people across the land to reject foreign rule. Independence, in both cases, meant that the international community welcomed a new member, legally equal to other independent states in the eyes of international law. The new leaders of both states also sought to use the glow of victory and the lessons they had learned in winning independence to play an important role on the world stage.

One claim that Nehru and Ben Khedda both put forth merits special attention. Both recounted histories in which the triumph of independence resulted from the urgent desire and long-standing struggle of a nation. A people long oppressed by colonial domination was now victorious. Yet as the Algerian's summons to "those who menace the necessary national cohesion and unity" and Gandhi's boycott of the ceremonies indicate, these shared moments of triumph were clouded by much more conflictual histories. Many former subjects of British India and French Algeria opposed independence, some because they were proud of their ties to a world-spanning empire and others because they *felt* British or French. Some Indians and Algerians had other preoccupations and had never shown any interest in independence. There were also those who had rejected colonial rule in pursuit of goals different from "national" independence. Some dreamed of a nation either larger or smaller than the Republic of India or the People's Democratic Republic of Algeria. Some still believed that links with the former colonizer could have been reformed. Others hoped that nonnational connections—for example, among the workers of the world; among "Africans," "Arabs," or "Asians"; or across the *umma* (the worldwide community of Muslims) or Christendom—would prove more important than divisions between "nation-states." It is important to recognize that India and Algeria—like every nation-state, whether the United States of America, Germany, or any of the states born through decolonization—struggled, at independence and after, to convince all of their people that what members of the "nation" shared was more important than what divided them. This remained true even with the recognition of the international community and even after schools began to teach ardently national histories.

Alongside the shared traits, there were also stark differences between Indian and Algerian independence, which the ceremonies in New Delhi and Algiers mirrored. Nonviolent civil disobedience had been a key strategy of the Indian National Congress campaign for liberation. This is a tactic in which protesters use peaceful means to violate laws they claim support injustice. Congress leaders themselves had established their authority by participating in British institutions and winning many of the elections the British authorized in India. American and British dignitaries were privileged guests at the independence ceremony, and Nehru and others presented this moment as a "tryst with destiny" that the people of India deserved due to their unique history. The FLN, by contrast, had defined itself in sharp opposition to previous Algerian nationalist movements. It had rejected any recognition of French law or French claims as a basis of negotiation, and it had embraced violent struggle as the only way to achieve victory. Whereas the French denied that there had ever been either an "Algerian nation" or a sovereign state, the FLN pledged to restore "Algerian sovereignty" to the Algerian nation (Document 19). Its legitimacy came from combat, on the ground and on the world stage, rather than from elections or debates in French forums. Algeria's new leaders were eager to present their triumph as emblematic of a revolutionary wave, which would sweep away all vestiges of colonialism and bring what many in 1962 called the "third world" to new prominence globally. Among the guests they invited to witness their victory were young would-be revolutionaries from around the Arab and African worlds, such as Yasir Arafat, a brash figure among Palestinian nationalists who would later lead the Palestine Liberation Organization (PLO), and Nelson Mandela, the South African leader of Umkhonto we Sizwe, the armed wing of the recently banned African National Congress (ANC): Both the PLO and the ANC modeled their claims and tactics on the FLN. Arafat accepted their invitation, but

Mandela preferred to leave the FLN camps where he had received military training to return to lead the struggle in his homeland. He was quickly arrested and in 1964 was condemned to life in prison.

Although the FLN shared the Indian Congress party's goal of national sovereignty, it must be said that in 1947 very few people—in London, Paris, New Delhi, Karachi, Algiers, and elsewhere—would have predicted that India and Pakistan were precursors to Algeria and the dozens of other states that gained independence in the years 1962 to 1965. In 1962, however, the connections became clear and seemed to extend to colonial situations across the globe. Today, this phenomenon is most often called *decolonization*. It encompassed actors and choices of all kinds, people from all stations of life and from around the world. To assess the period that stretches from just before India and Pakistan's "midnight hour" until three years after Algeria's armed victory over France, it is necessary to understand why we think of these local developments as part of one phenomenon, to sketch out the histories that led to the events of 1945 to 1965, and most important, to hear from some of the many voices of decolonization.

WHAT IS DECOLONIZATION?

The word *decolonization* seems to have first appeared in an 1836 French-language tract titled *Decolonization of Algiers*, in which the journalist Henri Fonfrède called on his homeland, the kingdom of France, to end its six-year occupation of territory in North Africa. Anticolonialists in Great Britain and on the continent continued to use the term through the 1850s. A few years later, however, as support for the conquest of new overseas colonies grew in popularity, *decolonization* disappeared from popular usage. In the late 1920s, a few Communists and social scientists revived the term. They did so either to analyze how British efforts to expand self-rule in India might lead to an international revolution of the working class, or to assess such developments as evidence of the decline of the West. In neither case did *decolonization* imply formal independence. In the 1930s, the work of Moritz Bonn, a proponent of the "decline of the West" argument, finally established the word among European scholars. Indeed, a number of historians, following Bonn's own claim, mistakenly identify the German economist as the inventor of the term. By the 1950s, European and American scholars and politicians alike hesitantly applied it to describe specific shifts in the exercise of sovereignty in particular territories. They did not see it as a general phenomenon. Like the French ethnologist Henri Labouret, who in 1952 published the first book with *decolonization* in its title (*Colonisation, colonialisme, décolonisation*), most Western scholars argued that "decolonizations" were wrongheaded, at least in the short term, and could be avoided through wise political choices made in Europe's imperial capitals. It was necessary to reform existing arrangements rather than get rid of them. In English, the word itself remained rather technical and little used. For example, it did not show up in the *New York Times* until 1959.[3]

Since then, however, *decolonization* has subsumed other terms describing what happened to European overseas empires after 1945, some of which were widely used, such as the aforementioned *national liberation, transfer of power*, and *end of empires*, as well as others that appear mainly in archived documents, such as the British India Office's evocations in 1945–1947 of *demission* (meaning "to withdraw from power"). Contemporary anticolonial critics proposed numerous descriptions as well. In the 1950s, the Senegalese essayist and historian Abdoulaye Ly described what he saw happening as "a ring of fire burning all along the Tropics," while in 1956 the French anthropologist Georges Balandier referred to "the insurrection of poor and dominated peoples" in order to argue that "this is the event that defines the twentieth century."[4] It was in French that the word *decolonization* first began to circulate widely. French-language writers began to use it regularly in reference to the Algerian War (1954–1962), the possible independence of French sub-Saharan colonies (1957–1960), and the Belgian Congo (1960). In popularizing it, they changed the term's meaning.

The most influential commentator on decolonization was the revolutionary theorist Frantz Fanon, in the articles and books he wrote while working with the FLN. Situating the people he described as "the colonized" in the history-making role that Marxists assigned to "the proletariat" or "the working class," Fanon summoned "the wretched of the earth" to take action (Document 25). Radical critics such as Fanon claimed that decolonization struggles could expose the violence and oppression inherent in European empire. Fanon also predicted that their actions to end colonialism might announce the birth of a new era when "the last shall be first."

Many scholars today employ the term *decolonization* to indicate merely the end of European states' formal colonial empires, whatever cause they may attribute it to. This "value-free" interpretation is intended to differentiate *decolonization* from other terms such as *national liberation*, which highlights the victory of anticolonialists, and *transfer of power*, which draws attention to shared decisions by colonial and anticolonial leaders. In the months leading up to Algerian independence,

French commentators who had strongly supported keeping the country French adopted this meaning of *decolonization*. They were the first to popularize its use in the singular: *decolonization*, rather than *decolonizations*, as in "decolonization is inevitable." If the decolonization of all colonies was inevitable, then Algeria's was not their fault: It was not linked to French choices or, for that matter, to the actions of pro-independence Algerians. That is to say, references to the "era of decolonization" can suggest that there was simply a structural process under way, a "tide of History" without human actors or individual decisions.

Other commentators, however, employ the term *decolonization* in order to explore and critique the gaps between what happened in terms of national sovereignty—the formal independence of so many new states—and what was hoped for in terms of freedom and fundamental change. This history explains why *decolonization*, although a term that can be used to describe various developments across human history, always carries with it some reference to the mid-twentieth-century end of direct European control of non-European territories. Some scholars date the beginning of this period from the British decision to establish a puppet monarchy in Egypt in 1921 (an attempt to neuter the growing anticolonial nationalist movement), but it is more usually thought of as beginning with Indian and Pakistani independence in 1947. The five-year high point of decolonization occurred between 1959 and 1963, when over thirty European dependencies became independent states. Later events, such as the independence of Portuguese colonies in 1973–1975, are often considered part of the same cycle. Most commentators include the end of white-minority rule in Rhodesia (now Zimbabwe) in 1979 as well, though there is some debate about whether the disappearance of apartheid in South Africa (and of South African rule over what became Namibia) in the early 1990s fits within the same narrative. Although roughly a dozen European overseas colonies remain today, most scholars consider 1997, when the United Kingdom returned Hong Kong to China, to mark the end of this "long" era of decolonization (see Map 3). It is in looking at the shorter era, from 1945 to 1965, however, that the meaning of decolonization becomes clear. In fact, the mid-twentieth-century upheaval around decolonization created the world we have today.

To understand decolonization, it is first necessary to realize that we are talking about something more than a historical epoch; the term also summons to mind a promise of sweeping change. When we refer to the "era of decolonization," centered on the period 1945 to 1965, we are defining it primarily as a period during which questions of national independence and political sovereignty for Asian, Pacific Islander, Caribbean,

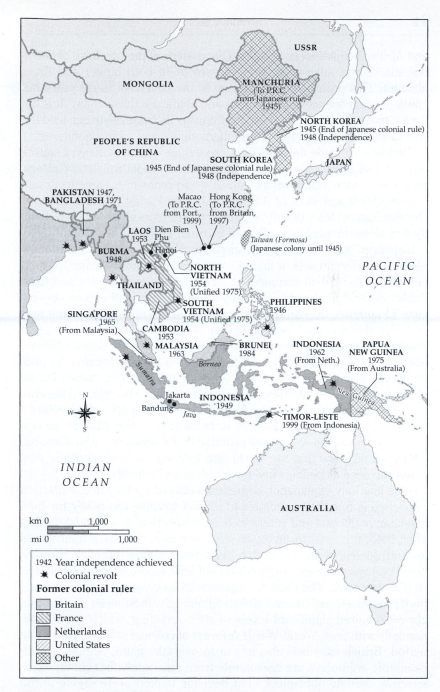

Map 3. *New States of Southeast Asia, 1945–1997*

11

and African peoples were at stake. Discussions of the "promise of decolonization," by contrast, encompass something both bigger and more abstract. This promise took shape over the course of those years but continues to influence world politics and political activists today: It is the dream that hard-fought efforts to end European colonialism can lead the way to worldwide liberation from unfair, unjust, and racist conditions.

Part of what made decolonization so unique—and, to many, a source of hope and inspiration—was that most of its most important actors, men and women, unknown as well as world renowned, came from outside the West and were of African, Asian, or Pacific Islander descent. Decolonization took place directly after the horrors visited upon humanity by two world wars that inflamed Europe. The arguments of anticolonialists drew strength from widespread and intense revulsion at the ideological claims and acts of fascist movements (notably Nazism), which celebrated the violent conquest of foreign lands and peoples and used explicitly racist arguments to justify mass murders and vicious oppression. In addition, decolonization occurred in the midst of the cold war, a conflict that was spearheaded by two countries led and run by men of European descent, the United States of America and the Union of Soviet Socialist Republics (USSR), and that seemed at once immune to public pressure and fated to lead to worldwide nuclear devastation. Public mobilization by everyday people, in which women who rejected the constraints of colonial laws were as visible as men going off to fight colonial armies, was critical to challenges to colonial rule. For all of these reasons, decolonization seemed to promise that a better day was dawning, which would show that the world had learned the lessons of the past about the need all peoples had for freedom and equality.

One less lofty explanation sometimes offered for why decolonization happened is that the economics of empire became too costly for metropolitan politicians and voters to bear. It seems clear in hindsight that after 1945, the need to invest in welfare states, refocus armed forces around nuclear weapons, and rebuild international prestige through novel policies made expenditures on old-style empires unfashionable as well as untenable. The French empire, with its geographic focus on vast underpopulated and inaccessible regions of sub-Saharan Africa, had always required significant levels of state spending, which grew exponentially with post–World War II reforms of colonial policy. In the same period, British expenses also began to overtake gains. Although such economic arguments are reasonable from our twenty-first-century perspective, they do not reflect what decision makers were saying at the time. It is noteworthy, for example, that in 1956 a well-known French journalist named Raymond Cartier used economics to advocate French withdrawal from sub-Saharan Africa. As Cartier wrote, "Black Africa for us is, like everything, a ledger. What is it worth? What does it cost? What does it offer? What hopes does it inspire? What sacrifices is it worth?" Yet for historians, it is more important that almost nobody in France took up this type of argument, which was mocked as "cartiérisme."[5] For Conservative British ministers in the 1950s, "prestige and economics were rather intimately linked."[6] They were convinced that pulling out of their costly West African colonies would give an impression of weakness that would lead to unstoppable decline, with catastrophic consequences for Britain's well-being (Document 1).

What is clear is that decolonization occurred when previously convincing arguments for empire came to seem unimaginable. While many of the elements that made this change possible were visible in 1945, it was not until the early 1960s that they became part of a larger and compelling case. On the one hand, it took a while for the implications of dramatic changes in world power politics to sink in and force political leaders to abandon previous positions and certainties. On the other hand, over the course of the 1950s a whole gamut of political projects premised on reforming existing ties between peoples rather than generalizing national independence were launched but then foundered (Documents 23 and 27–29). The "triumph" of decolonization came when formal independence began to seem the only response possible.

THE VARIETIES OF IMPERIALISM

During the era of decolonization, vast European overseas empires, largely built or consolidated in the late nineteenth century, almost completely disappeared. The late nineteenth century had witnessed the reinvigoration of assertions by political leaders and pundits throughout Europe that their countries should seek to control and govern other areas of the globe. This process of building or expanding an empire is called *imperialism*, a phenomenon that has occurred since ancient times and been pursued by peoples throughout the world. To distinguish it from previous European endeavors, the post-1860s era of European empire making is often called the *new imperialism*.

The new imperialism followed a period spanning several decades (1775–1824) when arguments critical of the direct rule of overseas lands had come to prominence among many European elites. This critique resulted from revolutions across the Americas that led to the independence of countries such as the United States, Haiti, Colombia, and Mexico. In the mid-nineteenth century, European proponents of new political and economic liberties ridiculed the idea that direct control over foreign lands made either political or economic sense. This, it must be emphasized, did not mean that imperial conquest stopped. In the very years when criticism of colonial rule flourished, the British claimed direct control over new territories in India and the French launched their conquest of Algeria. Concurrently, countries such as the United States and Great Britain used trade and other forms of economic leverage to influence, even control, other countries without formal intervention in their governments. Some scholars call such economic infringement "informal imperialism." This term is similar to what others—when speaking of developments after formal decolonization occurred—labeled "neocolonialism" (Document 39). In terms of actual expansion, that is, there was no "new imperialism," but rather a continuation. Since 1492, European states had expanded across oceans. Yet the imperial expansion that accelerated after the 1860s—and that then seemed to many to be something that any state that claimed to be "modern" had to pursue—marked a new age of European colonialism, far greater in scope than anything the world had seen before.

The term *colonialism* encompasses all of the diverse efforts by which colonizers seek to maintain or extend their rule over conquered territories and to benefit from this exercise of power. In the narrowest possible sense, this means that one state—the generic term is *metropole*, whether in reference to the United Kingdom, France, or any country with overseas colonies—legally defines a territory it has taken over as a colony, claims sovereignty over it, and administers it. In a colony, sovereignty—the ultimate authority over what decisions are made and through what political mechanisms—resides in the metropole. In the nineteenth and twentieth centuries, territories controlled by European and other states, though not called colonies, were effectively colonies, despite their legal status as protectorates, mandates, or extensions of the metropole (e.g., Algeria was legally defined as part of France from 1848 until 1962). By 1914, the United Kingdom, France, the Netherlands, Germany, Belgium, Italy, and Portugal—along with the non-European latecomers the United States and Japan—had divided up and were ruling almost all of Africa and South, Southeast, and East Asia, along with most of Oceania. In addition to territories they had seized under the ideological promptings of the new imperialism, Britain, France, the Netherlands, Spain, and Portugal also continued to control and govern previously conquered overseas lands. The most notable of these were areas where large-scale European settlement had taken place, such as Canada,

Australia, New Zealand, and South Africa (the "White Dominions" of the British Empire), as well as British holdings across South Asia, French Algeria, the Dutch East Indies (present-day Indonesia), Portuguese holdings on the African coast, and various Caribbean colonies.

The European conquest of these territories had been relatively easy, especially during the era of the new imperialism, when machine guns, telegraph lines and other forms of technology, and a disregard for African and Asian lives allowed European armies and their local allies to kill or devastate everyone who stood in their way. The Americans, when they seized control of the Philippines in 1898, and the Japanese, when they conquered Korea and Taiwan from 1876 to 1910, acted similarly. In most new colonies, however, very few colonizers actually remained in place to maintain control, and so they relied on local collaborators to exercise sovereignty. All sorts of reasons, from existing rivalries with other local people and leaders to new possibilities for power, prestige, knowledge, and wealth, led some of the conquered to put up with or accept—even respect or admire—the colonizing authorities. The opportunity to collaborate and gain benefits from colonial rule was the proverbial carrot. In every colony, there was also the stick: People who sought to resist colonial rule, or simply even unfair policies, suffered directly and brutally. Many spent time in prison or suffered bodily harm; quite often they were killed. Such repressive tactics gave support to complaints that colonialism, by treating colonized people as not fully human, did not bring civilization, but rather undermined it.

Still, as the twentieth century opened, colonialism continued to enjoy a largely positive reputation among European statesmen and among most of the Western writers who paid attention to it. Discussions centered less on exploiting the economic and military potential that empire offered than they had in previous decades. The concept of careful and respectful colonialism now overshadowed that of openly ambitious and adventuresome imperialism. Most arguments for maintaining European control in overseas territories asserted that it was good for all involved, the colonized as well as the colonizers.

INTERWAR EMPIRES: CRISIS AND CONSOLIDATION, 1918–1937

Retrospectively, a number of developments in the years between the end of the First World War (1918) and the beginning of the Second (1937) seem to have set the stage for decolonization. The evidence appears clearest for the biggest European empire of all. Throughout the interwar years, successive British secretaries of state publicly proclaimed that Britain saw its role as leading its dependencies to independence. Yet archival documents reveal that in closed-door discussions, virtually no British officials, colonial or metropolitan, either interpreted the policies they pursued as actually leading to this end or thought that they should. Rather, these officials believed that their country needed to control all its overseas territories, either as formal dependencies or through more informal means, and would continue to do so long into the future. This was true of most Europeans who thought about empire during this period. According to this perspective, the promise of political reforms (and the implementation of some) appeared to be a necessary means of maintaining imperial control.

There was, in fact, reason to think that certain empires had come out of World War I stronger than ever. On the ground, the Great War had extended European imperialism's reach even farther, taking in much of the Middle East. In 1914, the British transformed their informal domination of Egypt into a formal protectorate, while after 1918 France and Britain took over the Ottoman Empire's Arab provinces under the so-called mandate system that the new League of Nations established. In terms of everyday experience, both the French and British empires had deepened their contact with colonized people during the war. They had mobilized hundreds of thousands of these people to fight or to work in war industries and had extracted enormous amounts of materials from their colonies; this had entailed a new level of involvement of colonial administrations in the daily lives of the colonized. The great contribution that the overseas French and British dominions had made to victory provided clear proof of the benefits that colonies brought to the metropoles and, it seemed to European observers, of the willingness of colonial subjects to participate in the great mission of empire. These facts led countries that had empires to celebrate their diverse roles and growing unity, which supposedly characterized them. In those countries without an empire (post-1918 Germany) or with not enough of an empire (Italy, in the eyes of Mussolini's Fascist government), there were frequent debates about what could be done to remedy this situation.

As these developments suggest, after peace was declared, Europeans paid little attention to the fact that the Great War had also catalyzed new levels of discontent among colonized people and channeled growing numbers into newly organized forms of anticolonial action. Particularly important was how imperial war efforts had inspired a new awareness among certain colonial subjects of what and how much the colonizers demanded of them. This led some to begin to take full advantage of their already existing privileges. The self-governing British dominions of Australia and Canada, horrified by how British generals had wasted the lives of their soldiers, began to seek autonomy from the mother country. French citizens of the Four Communes in Senegal for the first time sent a deputy to the French National Assembly who had no European ancestry: Blaise Diagne promised to demand full recognition of all that Africans had contributed to the French victory.

Two other developments focused ongoing anticolonial protests on the goal of achieving national independence. First, diverse colonial nationalisms took root in the rich soil the bloody Great War had produced, a composite of revelation and repulsion: the recognition that European powers could be defeated and that the barbarism of European civilization could shock even Europeans. The second development was the reinvigoration of the nation-state model, as Europe's land-based empires—Austro-Hungary, Russia, and the Ottoman Empire—disappeared and the war-ending treaties embraced U.S. president Woodrow Wilson's call for the self-determination of all nations, put forward in his "Fourteen Points" speech, the peace proposal on which the truce had been based. The world, its preamble stated, must "be made safe for every peace-loving nation which, like our own, wishes to live its own life, determine its own institutions, [and] be assured of justice and fair dealing by the other peoples of the world as against force and selfish aggression." Wilson himself, a southerner with no interest in securing civil rights for African Americans, never even imagined that this principle could apply to people of color. Still, activists among many colonized people began to brandish his words to justify their struggle.

Nationalism had already established a foothold in Asia. The Philippine Revolution of 1896–1898, begun against Spanish rule and snuffed out by the Americans when they took over as colonizers, had given popular legitimacy to leaders who then continued to press the United States for independence in subsequent decades. The Japanese victory over Russia in the Russo-Japanese War of 1904–1905, the Chinese Revolution of 1911, and the Russian Revolution of 1917 had offered additional inspiration to some (often Westernized) elites to think in national terms and to imagine independence. After World War I, however, Asian nationalisms took on new importance. One key turning point came in 1919, when the Indian lawyer Mohandas Gandhi returned from South Africa and assumed leadership of the long-established Indian National Congress. He turned it away from charm campaigns aimed at influencing British rulers to loosen colonial oversight and toward a more aggressive and grassroots-based strategy to contest British rule.

The new importance of nationalism did not, in the interwar period, fully displace other organized forms of anticolonial activity, such as diverse movements of religious renewal (Muslim, Christian, Hindu, Buddhist), different forms of Pan-Africanism (some prescribing unity among all people on the African continent, others among all people of African descent), and various social and political movements, including antiracism initiatives, trade unionism, socialism, and communism. Nationalists did, however, prove very effective in integrating such approaches into their programs. Successful anticolonial nationalists were great syncretists, incorporating local traditions, slogans, and programs. Leading Indian nationalists, for example, had been educated in the English tradition and relied on European models of nationalism. Yet the independence movement there did not really take off until the Indian National Congress embraced Hindu catchphrases and explanations for its actions—in particular the nonviolent mass protests termed *satyagrahas* (from the Hindu word for "soul force")—and thus extended its reach across India and recruited large numbers of activists from rural areas and small towns.

Mass action—or, more accurately, the possibility of mass action—proved the most compelling means for anticolonialists to advance their cause. In the 1920s, this was particularly true in the British Empire, as imperial officials sought both to head off mass mobilization and to take advantage of concerns about the disorder produced by such activity to consolidate their control. A shared premise of both tactics was the disdain almost all European officials expressed toward what they derided as superstitious, backward, and lazy people. When Gandhi refused to wear a suit to his meetings with British officials, future prime minister Winston Churchill—encapsulating his widely shared attitude toward all who did not come from the West—characterized him as "a fakir of a type well known in the east, striding half-naked up the steps of the vice-regal palace."[7] Colonialists presumed that without European training and "civilization," their colonial subjects could not hope to govern themselves and that "natives" who had profited from Europe's beneficence would recognize this fact. Still, under the pressure of mass protests, Churchill and others did meet and negotiate with nationalists, even though they saw them as mere rabble-rousers.

Anticolonialism gained strength during the 1930s, when a worldwide depression undermined, in virtually every colony, any legitimacy that European rule had achieved. Economically underdeveloped and dependent, colonies suffered from the steep fall in prices for their primary goods, such as agricultural products. Local people placed the blame for falling commodity prices, lower wages, and increasing poverty on their colonial rulers. Concurrently, European governments made well-publicized decisions to protect their domestic constituents first, often to the clear detriment of their colonial subjects. Such choices called into question colonialist claims that European control brought economic development that colonized societies were unable to provide for themselves. Politically, the generalization of misery gave new impetus to nationalist movements in colonial societies—just as it did in the rest of the world. When worried colonial officials moved aggressively to impede political agitation, their actions often had the unexpected consequence of strengthening their local opponents. Indeed, they made radical options seem more attractive. This phenomenon was particularly marked in South and Southeast Asia. In the Dutch East Indies, for example, Dutch bureaucrats made panicked efforts to cordon off impoverished peasants from any outside contacts. This led to a new alliance among the diverse political factions that had developed within the small urban elite; these groups had previously been at loggerheads about what attitude to adopt vis-à-vis the colonial authorities. Forged against Dutch efforts, the new alliance was forthrightly critical of the authorities and starkly nationalist and had some success in reaching out to peasants.

Developments in subsequent years, when the depression's immediate devastation had passed, further undermined the credibility of those among the colonized who pursued collaboration rather than confrontation with the colonizers. In places such as India and French Indochina, as soon as colonial authorities loosened restrictions on political activities, pro-independence parties won elections or gathered strength, to the detriment of pro-colonial groups. This dynamic was encouraged, because in the rare instances when colonial authorities proposed reforms, it was under pressure from anticolonial activity associated with the radicals. They regularly ignored pleadings or proposals for reform from local advocates of collaboration. Another striking development was the new importance of radical trade union activism. In the aftermath of the depression, a wave of strikes against stagnant wages and the absence of social services swept through the British Empire. They began in 1935 in the Copperbelt, in present-day Zambia, where they spread from mines to local towns, then to railway workers in the Gold Coast (present-day Ghana) and ports along the East African coast. Their influence even resonated in work stoppages in the West Indies. Both Communist and Pan-African activists helped spread these actions across borders and oceans, establishing links that allowed local militants to believe that they were part of something larger.

In these same years, the actions and arguments of the fascist powers in Europe (Germany and Italy) and Japan also affected the practice of empire across the globe. Fascist regimes opposed egalitarianism and democracy and celebrated hierarchy and the cult of the "great leader." Fascists adhered to a racial mythology of national exceptionalism, rather than universal values, to explain why the biological destiny of one people was to rule over others. In the name of such fascist principles, these new regimes both sought to build their own empires and dusted off and redeployed classic explanations for imperialism. Japan's conquest of Manchuria in 1931 began a stunning series of colonialist expansions by what would become in World War II the Axis Powers: Japan conquered most of China after 1937; Italy conquered Ethiopia in 1935–1936; Germany conquered central, western, and then eastern Europe after 1939; and Japan expanded into Oceania and Southeast Asia after December 1941. In terms of territory and people affected, the decade 1931–1941 marked the farthest extension of colonial rule in history. Fascist leaders pushed to their extremes long-standing justifications for colonial rule that liberal democratic regimes had elaborated. They presented their states' colonial designs as preordained by destiny and history and necessary because of their racial superiority. Thus the Nazis called for *Lebensraum* (room to live); the Italian Fascists, invoking ancient Rome, spoke of *Mare Nostrum* ("our sea," i.e., the Mediterranean); and Japanese leaders promised to bring their "Asian brothers" out of Europe's shadows and into what they called the Greater East Asia Co-Prosperity Sphere.

Rendered in their crudest form, such arguments for empire lost much credit among outside observers and thus facilitated efforts by anticolonial activists. Also important to the post-1945 collapse of European empires, however, was that the Nazis largely pursued their empire within Europe, rather than overseas, and enacted racial laws and pursued racist violence against white people on the continent (especially Jews and Slavs) rather than against people of color abroad. Antifascist Europeans who had long supported or ignored overseas empires now claimed to recognize that something had to change.

WORLD WAR II: DECOLONIZATION
BECOMES IMAGINABLE

Once the United States entered World War II in 1941 on the side of the Allies (Great Britain, France, China, the Soviet Union, and others), American officials both targeted violent, racist imperialism as a key explanation for their fight against the Axis and amplified their disapproval of all forms of overseas colonialism, including that of their allies.

They repeatedly affirmed that all colonialism needed to end. In 1942, Undersecretary of State Sumner Welles, a top adviser to President Franklin D. Roosevelt, proclaimed, "The age of imperialism is dead."[8] Texts that explained why the Allies were fighting and laid the foundations for the postwar international order proposed (or so it seemed) the independence of colonized peoples as a goal. This was particularly clear in the Atlantic Charter, which British prime minister Winston Churchill and U.S. president Franklin Roosevelt signed in August 1941. Article 3 stated that signatories "respect the right of all peoples to choose the form of government under which they will live; and they wish to see sovereign rights and self government restored to those who have been forcibly deprived of them."[9] Here again, however, the situation at the time was far less clear than it seems in retrospect: The British and the governments-in-exile of France, Belgium, and the Netherlands all denied that such injunctions would apply to them. The British colonial secretary replied to Welles in July 1942 that "the British Empire is not dead, is not dying, it is not even going into decline," while Churchill affirmed on December 31, 1944, that "'hands off the British Empire' is our maxim" (Document 1).

At the end of World War II, despite the efforts of Churchill and his peers, the question of colonialism—and whether it could continue—emerged at the heart of international concerns. This resulted not from debates about empire among Western officials, but from two dramatic political developments. The first was the success of anticolonial nationalists in South and Southeast Asia and the Middle East, who confronted their colonizers with demands for immediate independence. The second was the new shape of world power politics that emerged from the war, namely: (a) new institutions that claimed to build a durable and effective international community, especially the United Nations, (b) the cold war, which introduced a sharp division in world politics, and (c) the dramatic decline in the influence of Europe's colonial powers. The first development produced a cascade of independence days across colonized Asia between 1947 and 1949, events that concretized the idea that the decolonization of certain colonial dependencies would lead to outright independence. Western officials, however, still refused to consider the possibility that all but a few colonies would soon become independent.

As the leaders of colonizing powers worked to make the most of the new world power politics, they claimed to reinvent their empires. They changed the legal status of "former colonies"—now called "dominions" or "overseas territories"—and pursued various reforms that, they believed, would maintain binding ties across the seas while answering calls for the "end of empire." The reactions of local leaders and people varied. Some pursued intense campaigns for independence. Others sought to take advantage of the new situation to increase their freedom and improve their conditions in the context of the "French Union" or the "British Commonwealth." For all, decolonization had emerged as a possibility, one that increased the pace of change in various ways across the colonized world. That decolonization would become a global phenomenon, however, seemed in no way inevitable.

NEW INTERNATIONAL CONNECTIONS

Between 1942 and 1949, nationalists in South and Southeast Asia and the Middle East used, in various combinations, mass actions, international pressure, armed struggle (or the threat of armed struggle), and the weak position of their colonial overlords to quickly obtain independence for all or part of the territory they claimed as their own. British India, by far the largest and richest European colony, provided the model. Nationalists there had developed a well-organized mass movement, the Indian National Congress, led by recognized and respected civilian leaders. The international credibility it had won in its push for freedom allowed the Congress to counter British maneuvers meant to extend colonial rule and ultimately to announce triumph on August 15, 1947.

World War II offered leaders of the Congress a fresh opportunity to highlight the hypocrisy of British resistance to Indian independence. The conflict also provided a context in which the organization's attempts to put pressure on colonial authorities proved particularly effective. In September 1939, when Viceroy Linlithgow declared that India, too, was at war with Britain's enemies, the Congress responded by arguing that "India cannot associate itself in a war said to be for democratic freedom when that very freedom is denied her," requesting instead a clear statement of the British government's war aims and immediate and significant moves toward self-rule.[10] Throughout the war, the Congress pursued mass protests in support of these demands, and by 1942 the British had agreed to establish full self-government when the war ended.

With relatively little conflict, and with the active collaboration of conservative local politicians, the United States granted the Philippines independence in 1946, and the British gave up sovereignty over Ceylon (later Sri Lanka) in 1948. In 1943, the Free French government-in-exile recognized Lebanese independence, while in 1946 the British recognized the full sovereignty of the government of Transjordan (present-day Jordan). These cases all buttressed the idea that the end of World War II and the defeat of fascism had inaugurated a novel international situation in which old ideas about empire and race had lost all credibility. Who should govern, and how, now had to be explained in reference to the goal of ensuring democracy and equality for all people.

The preeminent symbol of post–World War II hopes was the new United Nations, which came into being under U.S. guidance in 1945. The international echo of its establishment was significant, and the colonial question appeared to be one of the topics this institution would address. As with the Atlantic Charter of 1941 and Wilson's Fourteen Points of 1918, what allowed anticolonialists to link their dreams to the UN were the principles on which it was founded. Article 73 of its charter, which fifty-one states signed in 1945, most clearly captured anticolonialists' hopes, as it committed signatories "to develop self-government" (Document 2). The UN would become a central forum of international opinion on questions of empire. Its resolutions grew increasingly explicit in their condemnation of the continued existence of overseas colonies over the course of the years 1945 to 1965. In 1960, for example, the General Assembly passed a declaration, against the strong objections of the United States, the United Kingdom, France, and other Western countries, that "solemnly proclaim[ed] the necessity of bringing to a speedy and unconditional end colonialism in all its forms and manifestations" (Document 32). This was substantively different from what the UN Charter had announced, and it highlights how much expectations had changed in these fast-moving years: Things that seemed only possible in 1945 now appeared inevitable.

EUROPEAN EFFORTS TO REINVENT OVERSEAS COLONIALISM

Stirring words and new international organizations were not the main source of hope for those who, after World War II, looked to move beyond empire. Instead, it was the new shape of power politics. Colonizing states such as Britain and France had lost their long-standing place at the pinnacle and had been replaced by the two great superpowers, the United States and the USSR, both of which claimed to oppose colonialism. Each offered strong ideological and historical credentials to explain their opposition. The United States had been born in the first modern anticolonial revolution and was proud of that history, even if it had only begun explicitly to promote anticolonialism abroad in 1932, with the election of Franklin D. Roosevelt as president. This new approach became clear in dealings with the Philippines, the most important U.S. colony. Whereas previous administrations had rejected any discussion with local "agitators," Roosevelt sent officials to meet with Filipino nationalists in order to establish an explicit timetable for independence. (Unlike India or Pakistan, however, and like Egypt in 1922, the former colonizer remained a key player in local government for decades to come.) The Soviet Union's self-definition as a workers' state guided by Communist principles connected it to many of the most influential anticolonial activists and movements. The USSR's first leader, Vladimir Lenin, himself had penned one of the most frequently cited critiques of imperialism,[11] and the Soviet-run Comintern (Communist International, 1919–1943), which defined and spread Communist doctrine and organized Communist parties around the world, had provided training, resources, and political solidarity to anticolonial activists throughout the interwar period. Alongside U.S. actions during the war and the creation of war-ending treaties and postwar organizations, Soviet talk about the evils of imperialism seemingly offered another path for a quick end to colonialism. Anticolonialists often combined references to both superpowers, as the Vietnamese nationalist leader Ho Chi Minh did in declaring his country's liberation from French rule in September 1945 (Document 3).

Despite the many factors that contributed to discrediting European colonial rule in these years, it persisted in most places. The key reason was that at the end of World War II, every European colonial power saw the continuation of its control of overseas dependencies as deserved—as well as necessary for its political and economic well-being. British and French political leaders viewed holding on to their empires as fundamental to their respective claims to play a central role in the postwar political order. Led by Charles de Gaulle, French authorities shared Winston Churchill's aggressive rejection of outside pressure. In 1944, colonial administrators gathered in Brazzaville, the capital of French Equatorial Africa (now the capital of Congo), to map out the new principles and structures that would supposedly redefine the French empire. The formal declaration that came out of the Brazzaville Conference, however, stated that neither autonomy nor self-determination was among the options.

Even countries that had no illusions that they would remain international powers affirmed that their colonies still mattered. Dutch politicians, for example, saw reestablishing and maintaining their control of Indonesia as vital to their country's postwar renaissance. "The nightmare of the loss of Empire," as one historian describes it, troubled their hopes of creating a "new society out of the ruins" of defeat and occupation by the Nazis.[12] Most Italian leaders expressed shock when, under the terms of the Paris Peace Treaties of 1947, their country renounced all claims to the colonies it had ruled until the defeat of the Fascist regime. The famed liberal thinker and politician Benedetto Croce went before parliament to denounce this effort to take away regions that Italy "had acquired by her blood, and administered and elevated to civilized European standards by her genius and expenditure of her all too scarce financial resources."[13] Japanese leaders had a particularly difficult time accepting the end of their decades-long rule over Taiwan and, especially, Korea. Japan and the Republic of Korea (South Korea) did not establish diplomatic relations until 1965, despite pressure from the United States, their shared ally.

This desire to maintain imperial ties explains why, even as colonies such as India and the Philippines negotiated independence, transitions elsewhere in the immediate aftermath of World War II were more conflictual. In early May 1945, reacting to news that the war in Europe had been won, anticolonial demonstrators took to the street in the Syrian capital of Damascus. The protest remained largely peaceful until May 29, when French forces bombed the city, killing at least four hundred Syrians. In this case, international pressure (British prime minister Winston Churchill threatened to invade) forced the French to end the fighting, recognize Syrian independence, and withdraw their troops in April 1946.

The newly formed United Nations, which had called on the French to leave Syria in February 1946, soon was deeply involved in developments in neighboring Palestine as well. There the British—under intense pressure from U.S. president Harry Truman to accept the Zionist goal of the establishment of a Jewish state and unable to stop attacks by underground Zionist groups against Arab civilians, British institutions, and personnel—handed over control of their League of Nations mandate in Palestine to the United Nations. After strong lobbying by American politicians, and over the ardent opposition of its Arab members, the UN voted to divide Palestine into two states, one Arab and one Jewish. When the British pulled out on May 14, 1948, Zionist leaders proclaimed the State of Israel, which was attacked by its Arab neighbors the next day. By 1949, when all the parties involved had signed armistices, Israel had emerged victorious, no Arab state had been created in Palestine, and some 700,000 Arab refugees had been forced to leave their homes (Document 15 headnote).

Outside pressure and a state of war were also factors in other decolonizations in the late 1940s. After the Japanese defeat, the nationalist leaders Bogyoke Aung San in British Burma and Ahmed Sukarno in the Dutch East Indies sought to use the political authority and armed relays they had developed during the war (with the assistance of their Japanese occupiers) to force their European suzerains to recognize their countries' independence. Their aggressiveness won the day, but only after intense effort. Burma did not gain independence until 1948. In what would become Indonesia, Dutch forces launched a bloody military campaign to destroy the Republic of Indonesia, which nationalists had proclaimed in 1945. Only strong U.S. pressure finally led the Dutch to agree to independence in 1949. Even after this victory, however, the nationalists were unable to gain full control over the entire colony, as the Dutch held on to territory in New Guinea, which did not join Indonesia until 1962.

THE COLD WAR, LOCAL COLLABORATORS, AND THE SLOWING PACE OF CHANGE

Despite the roles that outsiders played in making Indonesian, Israeli, and Syrian independence possible, international diplomatic pressure to end imperialism waned in the late 1940s. One reason was that anticolonialism was not a priority for Soviet leaders in these years. As part of their 1930s decision to give primacy to the fight against fascism, European Communists already had muted their support for immediately ending colonial rule. After 1945, the obsession of Soviet dictator Joseph Stalin with protecting his country from threats in Europe led the Soviets to play little active role in fomenting anticolonial struggles. More important, U.S. anticolonialism, which Roosevelt had articulated emphatically and U.S. diplomats had maneuvered to assert in the UN and vis-à-vis their allies, quickly foundered. Between 1947 and 1951, the emergence of the cold war led U.S. policymakers to focus on strengthening their European allies against the perils of Soviet invasion and domestic Communist parties. This made it easy to ignore nationalist demands from colonized people, particularly in Africa, and even actively to support the continuation of European colonial control.

The two important Asian territories that did not see the end of colonial rule in the immediate post–World War II years, British Southeast Asia (present-day Malaysia and Singapore) and Indochina (Vietnam, Laos, and Cambodia), eventually became important sites of conflict in the

emerging cold war (see Map 3, page 11). Whereas Indonesian nationalists' role in crushing Communist activities had encouraged U.S. efforts
to pressure the Dutch to leave, the growing importance of communism
for Vietnamese nationalists had the opposite effect on U.S. policy toward
Indochina. This shift was particularly blatant, given that President
Roosevelt himself had repeatedly identified French rule there as typify-
ing the worst excesses of colonialism: financial neglect, repression of
political activity, and the consolidation of a feudal-style agricultural system. The British quickly responded to the U.S. turnabout, using their
1948 declaration of the Malayan Emergency, made in the name of coun-
tering a Communist insurgency (1948–1960), to sideline their earlier
policy of extending autonomy in the region. The British also began to
argue that their continued control of Asian colonies was meant to build
up local nationalisms as a bulwark against the spread of communism.
Throughout this era, Western and indigenous defenders of maintaining
colonial ties to Europe constantly invoked concerns about communism.

It was not just Europeans who wanted to hold on to imperial rule. This
was most clearly the case for colonized people who had benefitted from
their collaboration with European authorities. The king of Travancore,
India's southernmost territory and one of the so-called princely states
that British rulers had left in place, offers one picturesque example. In
the years before 1947, Chithira Thirunal had worked with the hereditary leaders of many other states, first to prevent India's independence
and then to avoid incorporation into the future republics of India and
Pakistan. It was an assassination attempt by Communists on his prime
minister, along with repeated British assurances that many of his privileges (and his family's wealth) would be maintained, that finally set the
stage for union with India.

More typically, however, many common people preferred the stability of imperial rule to the threat of upheaval, or quite simply the rulers
they knew rather than the unknown figures who might take the current rulers' place. In post-1945 Vietnam (as in other dependencies), for
example, although many men and women who had been educated in
colonial schools became harsh critics of European rule (Document 4),
others preferred to work within the system. The same was true among
those with personal or familial ties to the British or French armed
forces: While some veterans played key roles in anticolonial movements, others became stalwarts of the existing regime. In most places,
we must remember, large numbers of people had little or no contact
with either the colonizing state or critics of colonial rule, and many gave
no indication they had commitments either way. This "silent majority"

often seemed like the bedrock that would allow existing (i.e., colonial) institutions and governments to withstand the shifting currents of post-war upheaval. That was certainly the opinion of many colonial officials and settlers of European origin in Rhodesia, Algeria, Kenya, and Angola, who argued that what was necessary was a strong hand and an unwavering defense of the status quo, not "reforms," which would signal weakness (Document 33). Despite this view, standing still was not an option for most European leaders.

The colonial powers tried all sorts of approaches to hold on to what empire they still ruled. For several years following World War II, such efforts seemed quite likely to work. This was in large part because some colonized people bought into the new approaches. One thing that made continued collaboration newly palatable was that in the aftermath of fascism's defeat, European leaders felt compelled to expunge racial claims from their arguments in favor of imperialism (Document 6). Indeed, they presented the maintenance of ties forged in empire as the best way to fight racism and increase equality.

After Britain's left-wing Labor party took power in 1945, party leaders took pride in hewing to a middle path, which avoided both the old-style imperialism still popular among Conservative leaders (such as Churchill) and the ardent anticolonialism of the far left. A prominent minister announced in 1946 that his colleagues were "great friends of the jolly old Empire." Yet the government preferred to emphasize that its commitment to extending egalitarian politics to all British subjects had produced something wholly different from what had existed before. As one Labor party publication proclaimed in 1948, "Imperialism is dead, but the Empire has been given new life."[14] Against strong opposition from British settlers and authorities on the ground, London tentatively extended eligibility for certain welfare programs to African workers in Kenya. At the same time, some leaders sought to reinvent the Commonwealth— which had been inaugurated in the 1920s to link autonomous "White Dominions" (Canada, Australia, New Zealand, and South Africa) to the British crown—to include states with few inhabitants with European ancestry, whether the republics of India and Pakistan or other, current colonies. Most anticolonial nationalists, it was hoped, would be satisfied with the extension of autonomy and participation in the Commonwealth rather than independence. In reforms that paralleled but went further than those of the British, French legislators after 1945 proposed a new federal-style system, termed the French Union, to knit together and govern the French republic and its empire. These decisions had some significant effects, with the end of laws authorizing forced labor the most obvious and successful campaigns by local trade unionists for minimum wage laws and other social rights for workers in French West Africa the most promising.

Both the United Kingdom and France bolstered their overseas efforts to transform their empires with redefinitions of national belonging. They changed laws to create a shared identity between "metropolitans" and overseas "compatriots." They also offered new possibilities for people from the empire to enter the metropole and to live and work there (Document 38). The 1946 constitution of the Fourth Republic created French Union citizenship, which put all French nationals and colonial subjects in the same category, eliminating the latter term altogether from official language. As part of an effort to solidify the connections between Britain and what remained of its empire, the Nationality Act of 1948 affirmed that all inhabitants of the empire, all of which was now termed the Commonwealth, had British nationality, with equal rights to entry into and employment within the United Kingdom.

Between 1946 and 1962, taking advantage of these and other new rights—and of Britain's desperate need for workers to staff the postwar economic boom—some 400,000 people of color moved to Great Britain from the colonies (Document 38). At the same time, Britain also acted to cement connections by encouraging Britons to emigrate elsewhere in the Commonwealth. Hundreds of thousands of them did so, many moving to the "White Dominions," but significant numbers also settling in Kenya and other colonial possessions. The Portuguese government, under the dictatorship of Antonio de Oliveira Salazar, also sought to use emigration to invigorate its overseas empire. As a result, the white population of Angola quadrupled between 1940 and 1960, while that of Mozambique tripled in the same period (see Map 2, page 5).

THE RISE OF ANTICOLONIAL RADICALISM

By 1950, changing international conditions and reform campaigns convinced many European observers that the contagion of independence had been contained. Yet as in 1945, developments on the international stage and on the ground continued to raise questions about colonialism and to link it to other forms of profound injustice. The most important of these were racism and poverty.

The obvious connections between pro-colonial arguments and Nazi and fascist racist claims had motivated British and French reforms. Even Portuguese leaders, who did little to change official policies in their African colonies, suddenly embraced arguments that "Portuguese culture" rejected racism and encouraged racial mixing. These gestures did not stem surging demands that racism be analyzed, condemned, and combated (Document 27). In terms of analysis, one of the most influential interventions came from a group of prominent social scientists, who seized the public platform offered by the new United Nations Educational, Scientific, and Cultural Organization (UNESCO). In 1950, they invoked the authority of the UN Charter and UNESCO's founding principles to explain their publication of the official UNESCO "Statement on Race," which argued that science had demonstrated that "race" is a social construct, not a biological phenomenon (Document 6). The statement provoked intense and very public debates among social scientists, and between biologists and anthropologists. These took place against the backdrop of campaigns for African American freedom and civil rights, which had unleashed international discussions about the racial situation in the United States. As critics drew comparisons between blacks in the United States and people of color in colonial situations, leaders and diplomats on both sides of the Atlantic came under pressure to respond.

Alongside racism, critics frequently linked the continued existence of dramatic economic inequality and profound poverty to colonial rule. Despite incremental reforms, many people in the colonies were increasingly aware that decisions about their lives remained in the hands of outsiders; as result, they argued, colonialism was responsible for their difficult economic conditions. Criticisms of the stark economic divide between metropoles and colonies, and between European settlers and native inhabitants of the colonies, also flourished. The Algerian author Mohammed Dib's powerful novels, such as *L'Incendie* (*The Fire*), published in 1954, presented readers with devastating depictions of how the colonial state's disregard for the welfare and dignity of local people led to famine (Document 18). The French anthropologist Germaine Tillion, in an attempt to explain the decline in rural Algerians' living standards that she witnessed between the 1930s and the 1950s, argued that French rule had produced the "pauperization" of the Arab and Berber populations.[15]

Such intellectual arguments about unfair conditions help explain why, in the early 1950s, anticolonial activity did more than continue; in growing numbers of colonies, it grew more agitated (Document 16). Indeed, as European promises of reform seemed to displace plans for independence, radicalism among anticolonialists increased. In 1948, for example, the Kenya African Union (KAU) organized women to peacefully protest British efforts to "reform" agricultural practices (Document 11). A few years later, the growing anger of thousands of Kenyans (notably among the politicized Kikuyu people) that British control over African land and lives had strengthened, rather than abated, encouraged the radicalization of their movement (Documents 12 and 13).

Whether increased radicalism resulted from or produced violence is unclear. Violence was central to decolonization, as it had been to colonialism, although the intensity, effects, and constancy of violence, both actual and threatened, differed dramatically among colonies and over time. The reportedly "peaceful" British withdrawal from India provoked massive population movements, as people sought to reach or flee the territorial confines of India or Pakistan. Partition was accompanied by unbearable levels of violence: Verifiable data is unavailable, but estimates begin at some 200,000 dead; credible claims indicate that perhaps as many as 2 million died.[16] In 1946, French troops sought to crush the Democratic Republic of Vietnam, which had proclaimed its independence on September 2, 1945. Until 1954, when the Treaty of Geneva led to the French leaving Indochina, some 75,000 French soldiers and 18,000 Vietnamese troops allied with France died; the number of Vietnamese killed by French forces is unknown, although estimates commonly begin at 400,000. Vietnam was typical of other conflicts: In virtually every case, defenders of colonial rule caused significantly more deaths and casualties than their opponents, even as they collected precise figures for those who suffered on their side and often only vague estimates for those they victimized.

Nonetheless, a substantial amount of public attention at the time focused on the violence wrought by anticolonialists, which critics defined as unprecedented in its barbarism and cruelty. When protests against French rule in Sétif, Algeria, turned violent on Victory in Europe Day (May 8, 1945), with crowds targeting European settlers and killing about one hundred, even Communist deputies in the French parliament suggested that nationalist "outlaws" had been provoked by Nazis. No evidence exists to support this, however. Between 1950 and 1956, a rebellion that coalesced out of struggles over land and demanded that all "whites" leave Kenya resulted in the deaths of close to two thousand African civilians, two hundred members of the police and British armed forces, and thirty-two white settlers. The British government referred to the rebels as the "Mau Mau," a name of uncertain origin that became synonymous with vicious, uncontrolled savagery (Documents 10–13). In both Algeria and Kenya, colonial troops responded to so-called anticolonial barbarity with overwhelming force. The French army killed thousands of Algerians over several weeks, and the British army pursued a campaign that involved interrogating and imprisoning huge numbers of

Africans, which resulted in the destruction of the rebellion and tens of thousands of dead Kenyans.

Anticolonial violence undeniably contributed to keeping debates about colonialism on the front burner of world opinion. This was true for both the so-called Mau Mau rebellion in Kenya and the spectacular victory of North Vietnamese armed forces over the French at Dien Bien Phu in the spring of 1954 (which forced Paris to agree to the Treaty of Geneva). Such violence also contributed to the spread of anticolonial politics within the colonies, through fear of nationalist radicals, on the one hand, and through identification with them, on the other. The latter usually far outweighed the former, largely because the response of colonial authorities was always vastly disproportionate: Inevitably, large numbers of local people who had no or only marginal previous involvement with anticolonialists suffered or died.

THE INTERNATIONAL POLITICS OF DECOLONIZATION

Another factor that kept the question of colonialism on the international agenda was the active efforts of newly independent states. India and Indonesia, the largest states to decolonize since 1945, presented themselves as models for still colonized people. Other states also asserted their status as newly emancipated from Western colonialism, including the (Communist) People's Republic of China, which had come into being in 1949 after a violent revolution, and Egypt, where a revolt in 1952 ousted the king and placed Gamal Abdel Nasser in charge. Nasser later asserted that Egypt's revolution was the start of true independence from colonialism (Document 14). The role of such independent states in supporting anticolonial movements varied dramatically, but it was in working together that they had the greatest effect.

In the same years that British and French leaders were trying to invent new forms of imperial unions—commonwealths, federations, and the like—critics of colonialism mobilized across territorial boundaries. Immediately after 1945, preexisting transnational forums such as the Pan-African Congress, which had begun in 1919, took on new importance in linking anticolonial struggles, as did labor unions and the international Communist movement (Document 5). By the 1950s, however, it was the third world, a continent-spanning entity, that began to be described as the most important venue in which to build international connections and to plan for a better future. In a 1952 magazine article, the French social scientist Alfred Sauvy invented the term *third world* to explain his argument that there were currently three worlds: industrialized capitalist states (Western, or pro–United States), industrialized socialist states (Eastern, or pro–Soviet Union), and the rest of the world (Document 7).

In August 1955, the leaders of twenty-nine newly independent African and Asian states met for the Asian-African Conference at Bandung, Indonesia (also known as the Bandung Conference). The most important message to emerge from this gathering was that these states had a shared understanding that colonialism had to end and that they were willing to do what they could to achieve that goal. This idea resonated internationally, thanks to the substantial coverage the meeting garnered from journalists and commentators (Documents 8 and 9).

In this mid-1950s context, the United States and the Soviet Union again turned their attention to the colonial question. Each sought to draw what the Indian leader Jawaharlal Nehru termed the "nonaligned" countries of the world away from the other, an effort that the growing number of UN debates on colonialism made strikingly visible. Each also sought to check attempts by the Chinese to position themselves at the ultimate defender of third world causes (Documents 9 and 36). U.S. policymakers had become increasingly certain that no further European state was likely to "fall" to communism. Concurrently, U.S. analysts began to give increasing attention to the destabilizing effects of struggles for decolonization in Africa. They were concerned over Soviet influence in these movements. With the election of John F. Kennedy to the presidency in 1960, the United States once again began to give strong verbal support to ending overseas colonial rule. In 1957, even before he won the presidency, Kennedy had used his first speech before the U.S. Senate to denounce French efforts to prevent Algerian independence. The Soviets, too, increasingly embraced struggles they had previously dismissed as merely "nationalist" or "bourgeois." In the early 1960s, Soviet premier Nikita Khrushchev spoke enthusiastically about the "revolutionary" surge of national liberation movements and reoriented Soviet foreign policy in their direction.

ALGERIA'S DECOLONIZATION

One struggle over colonialism in particular garnered an enormous amount of attention. Its instigators called it the Algerian Revolution; others spoke of it as the Algerian War; French officials soft-pedaled it as "events in Algeria." It merits special attention because over the eight bloody years of this conflict, the belief that the decolonization of all colonies was inevitable became a widely shared assumption. In 1954, international opinion regarded Algeria as exceptional—wholly unlike other overseas dependencies, not even a real colony—but by 1962 it had become widely cited as the preeminent example of why and how decolonization took place. Both views were dubious, yet each directly affected events on the ground in Algeria and elsewhere.

When the FLN began its armed struggle for independence on November 1, 1954 (Document 19), French politicians and Western journalists almost universally argued that Algeria was very different from other overseas territories, namely those that were moving toward or had recently won independence: Algeria *was* France (Documents 20 and 23). This was legally the case, although it was the presence of almost one million French settlers that made it plausible. The French dominated economic life (although most French settlers were far poorer than most people in France); some families had been there for several generations; and in some towns and the biggest cities (Algiers, Oran), they comprised the majority. The close to eight million inhabitants of Arab or Berber background—whom French laws referred to as "Muslims"—were, since the 1946 signing of the constitution of the Fourth Republic, "French citizens." Yet only a small percentage of them had the same rights as their European compatriots; the rest had far fewer rights, and the majority lived in miserable conditions that had only worsened in recent years (Documents 18 and 21).

Like all nationalists, anticolonial or not, the FLN asserted that it represented the nation and that all true Algerians shared a culture—in this case, one anchored in a coming together of Arab and Berber roots, shaped by Islam and its values, and united through the Arabic language and by a desire for liberty. For these reasons, Algerians needed their own state. Independence, the FLN argued, would allow Algerians to establish new ties with their Arab and Muslim neighbors in North Africa and the Middle East. Most French voices rejected these arguments. Only a handful of people in the metropole were willing to entertain the idea that there was an "Algerian nation" or that there had ever been an Algerian state. Many argued that the FLN's nationalism was simply a combination of anti-European racism and Muslim fanaticism. Some, including the center-left government that was in power when the war for independence broke out, agreed that France should do more to remedy the economic and social injustices in Algeria and to extend new rights to Muslims there. Yet most of these people also thought that only France could improve Algerians' lot and that independence would have disastrous effects on Algerians as well as on France.

Despite the FLN's claims that it represented the people and that the people were rising up en masse to kick out the occupiers, many Algerians did little or nothing at first to support the rebels. Many members of the European-educated elite remained attached to France. In addition, a substantial number of anticolonial Algerians did not recognize the FLN's authority. Some looked to the Algerian Communist party, and others remained loyal to other nationalist organizations. An even larger number of Algerians had no opinion about the FLN at all and, more important, either were unwilling to challenge the existing government or preferred stability to radical change. Many, it is important to recognize, made choices based on local conditions, personal or group loyalties, or family ties, rather than on a settled opinion about French rule or FLN politics.

The FLN recognized that to win, it needed Algerians to recognize its authority, even if they were not actively involved in the independence movement. Violence was key to achieving this goal. France had ample means, both military and financial, to punish resistance of any kind and to reward any form of loyalty. The FLN argued that given French power and their record of brutally repressing nationalist activity, it had no choice but to use violence. Violence could create the conditions that would allow Algerians to express their support for independence.

The forms of FLN violence changed over time. In the first months of the rebels' activities, they claimed that the only civilians they targeted (as opposed to military or police forces) were identified "traitors" or colonial agents. Their definition of traitors, it must be noted, was broad and included Algerians who worked with the French government, as well as anticolonial activists who rejected FLN injunctions to join the movement. The FLN's deadly combat with a rival nationalist group, the Algerian National Movement (known by its initials in French, MNA), continued for years and included the killing by each side of the other's civilian supporters. In August 1955, certain groups of *moudjahidine* (fighters) — whom French authorities called *fellaghas* (bandits) and, later, *hors-la-loi* (outlaws) — began to target the European civilian inhabitants of so-called colonist centers. Their goal was to encourage or force local Muslims into a new level of complicity with the rebels. Locals became complicit if they participated in the attacks or, more often, if they just remained silent. Even more frequently, French retribution convinced them that they had to align with the FLN. Eliciting such retribution was another goal of FLN violence.

Compared with the rebels' actions, French violence was far greater in scope and effects. The systematic use of torture on Algerians suspected of any form of complicity typified the French reaction to FLN actions. Being Muslim and in the way was often all it took to provoke suspicion (Document 22). Claude Bourdet, one of France's most widely read journalists, warned as early as January 1955 that French soldiers were turning into a "Gestapo," a reference to the Nazi secret police.[17] Despite such criticism, the military justified illegal techniques with the claim that they were needed to prevent "terrorism." Archival evidence, however, clearly shows that the same techniques were in widespread use against Algerians long before FLN violence began. This evidence also indicates that torture was usually an ineffective intelligence tool, as victims, desperate to end their agony, were more likely to say what they thought the torturers wanted to hear than what they knew to be true. Just as with the army's use of collective punishment—destroying villages and confiscating land in cases of suspected support for the FLN—the use of torture aimed to deter people from supporting the FLN and to deprive the organization of the support and supplies it needed to conduct its campaign within Algeria.

The FLN explicitly embraced terrorism in 1956, avowedly in response to French collective punishment against Muslim civilians: It would expand its strikes against outposts of the colonial state to include all European civilians in order to create terror and change French policies (this was how FLN leaders themselves defined "terrorism"; for French authorities, the term had no specific meaning, and could be used in reference to any form of violence they disagreed with). In practice, though, FLN forces killed far more Muslims in Algeria—over 16,300—than Europeans. Critics of the rebels, however, focused more on the types of violence than the scope. The French government and other supporters of French Algeria produced photographs and testimonials of so-called FLN terrorism, and French and international media fixated on incidents in which guerrillas had castrated or beheaded soldiers or civilians. The paucity of images of state-sponsored acts of violence certainly facilitated this wartime focus on FLN atrocities.

By the war's end, an estimated 3,000 European civilians were dead from the fighting, as were nearly 18,000 French soldiers. The number of Algerian dead was more uncertain. Estimates from the independent Algerian government reached more than 1 million, while more recent demographic and archival studies suggest that between 350,000 and 570,000 Algerians died as a result of the war. At least 250,000 Algerians were direct casualties of French violence; famine and disease led to the remaining deaths.

Debates about torture and terrorism played an important role in making the war a topic of international concern. The internationalization of the conflict was something that the FLN had made a key goal and that the French government sought eagerly to avoid. Early on, the French had some success in preventing this from happening. Since both the United States and the Soviet Union saw France as a crucial player in the cold war—a U.S. ally yet open, as the Soviets appreciated, to acting independently to advance its interests—neither contested French arguments that Algerian events were domestic affairs. Yet ongoing violence and FLN public outreach campaigns began to change this dynamic, and when the 1955 Bandung Conference made Algeria's independence a central topic of concern and agreement, it aided FLN efforts to present independence as a moral imperative. French efforts to focus attention on FLN violence became less and less effective, while critics of French brutality gained in influence. This shift in attitudes was particularly visible in the Battle of Algiers, which began with FLN terrorist attacks in the city in late 1956 and ended after French forces crushed the last cell of FLN fighters in late 1957. The French victory, which owed much to the torture and intimidation of Algerians, turned out to be a public relations debacle. It was one of many.

In 1956, French anger at the assistance the Egyptian government was giving to the FLN (including intense propaganda broadcasts into Algeria via the Voice of the Arabs radio station) contributed to France's decision to join the British and Israeli attack on Egypt, ostensibly to "liberate" the recently nationalized Suez Canal. While the invaders had initial success, no one on the international stage accepted the Europeans' pretension that they had intervened to help the Israelis only after the invasion had occurred. Instead, it was clear that they had been party to a plan to humiliate Nasser's government and to reaffirm British and French power in the Mediterranean. When U.S. president Dwight D. Eisenhower joined Soviet premier Nikita Khrushchev in demanding that the aggressors withdraw from Egyptian territory without conditions, the British quickly acquiesced and the French were forced to follow. Rather than reinforce their authority, the Suez Crisis seemed to prove that neither France nor the United Kingdom had the capacity to act in the world without U.S. assistance (Document 14).

In 1958, events in Algeria precipitated what many termed a coup d'état in France itself, which forced the existing French government out of power. A new government, led by General Charles de Gaulle, established a new constitution and the Fifth Republic. De Gaulle committed his government to making Algeria fully part of France. Both the United States and the Soviet Union responded positively to de Gaulle's arrival in office, the former pleased that its ally was now led by a firm hand, the latter hopeful that de Gaulle's commitment to the revival of French power would lead him to move away from the United States. De Gaulle's Algerian policy was a serious blow to FLN hopes for independence. Yet the organization soon recovered its footing—not militarily, as French tactics effectively disabled the organization within Algeria, but in terms of growing signs that Algerians yearned for independence and of increasing clamor from other countries and in international public opinion that Algeria's decolonization was inevitable. It came in 1962.

By the time of Algeria's independence, the debate between anticolonial and pro-colonial voices seemed largely settled. European claims that there were multiple forms of colonialism and multiple paths out of the current situations in colonized territories increasingly appeared simply irrational. With the collapse of the French Union and the success of the independence movement in Ghana (formerly the British Gold Coast) under the charismatic leadership of Kwame Nkrumah in 1957, even those anticolonial politicians or union activists who had sought to take advantage of opportunities provided by postwar French and British reforms embraced the necessity of independence. Only after independence was achieved, they now agreed, could new forms of interstate cooperation emerge. Even in the Belgian Congo, where almost no anticolonial militants existed and which had seemed destined to remain under Belgium's control, independence came to seem an immediate necessity (Documents 28 and 29).

Within just a few years, most European states left their last important colonies, with Belgium leaving the Congo in 1960, the Netherlands accepting Indonesia's claims to Dutch New Guinea in 1962, and the United Kingdom freeing Kenya in 1963. European leaders presented these decisions, which they had energetically fought to prevent, as obvious. British prime minister Harold Macmillan's widely reported "Wind of Change" speech, which he delivered in February 1960 before the parliament of the Union of South Africa, announced and laid out rationales for the end of Britain's support for white-minority rule of territories in its Commonwealth and for the independence of all colonized African territories (Document 30). Charles de Gaulle and other French politicians affirmed that Algeria's independence was part of the "tide of History" named decolonization, an inevitable development that wise politicians could only recognize, not alter (Document 24).

THE LEGACIES OF DECOLONIZATION

The documents collected here make clear how, over twenty years, from 1945 to 1965, something that seemed possible but open to debate—and that, for some on all sides, seemed worth fighting long and hard for—came to seem obvious and necessary to most people around the world. Yet 1965 did not by any means mark the end of the struggle for decolonization. Two groups of countries stood out in subsequent years for their blatant rejection of what anticolonial activists claimed were the lessons of the era of decolonization. Portugal's African colonies (Angola, Mozambique, Cape Verde, Guinea-Bissau) remained under increasingly tight colonial rule, which the country's authoritarian leaders insistently argued was in the interest of their African "compatriots" (Documents 33–35). Meanwhile, the former British colonies of South Africa (in 1961) and Rhodesia (in 1965) both broke political ties with Britain in the name of defending their "white African" (or European) cultures; both established a formally democratic government that excluded "black Africans" and most other non-Europeans (as well as "mixed-race" people) from citizenship, political rights, and most other rights, such as freedom of movement (Document 31). In response, the main antiracist and anticolonial political groups in all of these countries turned to violence. South Africa's decades-old African National Congress (founded in 1912) set up an armed wing in 1961, while the Mozambique Liberation Front (FRELIMO, for its initials in Portuguese, founded in 1962) announced its acceptance of the need for armed struggle in 1964.

Israel was another country that emerged as a focus of international discussions of anticolonialism and decolonization over the course of the 1960s. In 1965, a nationalist group called the Palestinian National Liberation Movement, known as Fatah, for its initials in Arabic, began to conduct armed attacks on Israeli positions. Its leader, Yasir Arafat, who had trained with FLN forces in Morocco (alongside South Africa's Nelson Mandela), presented the Palestinian struggle against Israel as wholly anticolonial (Documents 15 and 37). While most Western countries were publicly critical of the continuation of Portuguese colonialism and of the policies embraced by South Africa and Rhodesia (even as they worked with these countries in the name of fighting the Soviet bloc), their leaders rejected depictions of Israel as a colonial power. They also harshly condemned as terrorists all anticolonial groups that embraced armed struggle, such as the ANC, FRELIMO, and certain Palestinian groups.

In turn, many of these groups were very critical of the West, notably the United States, which they accused of imperialism or neocolonialism. This was true even though most of the groups were explicitly anti-Communist. The South African ANC leader Nelson Mandela analyzed this situation during his 1964 trial for (among other charges) "violent revolution" and "furthering the objects of communism." He asserted that "it is perhaps difficult . . . to understand why experienced African politicians so readily accept communists as their friends. But to us the reason is obvious. Theoretical differences amongst those fighting against oppression is a luxury we cannot afford at this stage. What is more, for many decades communists were the only political group in South Africa who were prepared to treat Africans as human beings and their equals." Mandela claimed that "in the United Nations and other Councils of the world the Communist bloc has supported the Afro-Asian struggle against colonialism and often seems to be more sympathetic to our plight than some of the Western powers."[18] For some in the West, this willingness to compromise or work with Communists made it impossible to support anticolonialism and cast into doubt the sincerity of anticolonialists' claims. *Nonaligned* or *third world*, they argued, really meant *pro-Soviet* (Document 36).

Over the course of the 1960s and after, however, other people looked to continuing anticolonial struggles as models for political action that appeared quite distinct from communism, and certainly from the Soviet bloc. Civil rights leader Martin Luther King Jr. in the United States, people fighting for "gay liberation" in France, and others working for minority rights in Spain took anticolonial struggles as inspirational models. Others turned to more radical or violent aspects of the struggle against colonialism to explain their own policies, such as the Provisional Irish Republican Army, which began an armed campaign against British rule of Northern Ireland in 1969, and the Black Panthers, who spoke of the "internal colonialism" suffered by U.S. blacks to explain their acceptance of armed resistance. Numerous theories that emerged in the context of decolonization grew in importance for academics and political activists seeking to describe the world. Among the most influential were Frantz Fanon, who analyzed the conflict between colonized and colonizers (Document 25), and Kwame Nkrumah, whose description of neocolonialism allowed commentators to explain why political decolonization—the end of direct rule by Western countries over other parts of the world—had not led to complete liberation, or even local control of economic development (Document 39).

It is this complicated, even paradoxical heritage that makes decolonization, still today, a touchstone for so many discussions. The mid-twentieth-century anticolonial victories and the principles that anchored the promise of decolonization remain compelling and attractive to many; the deception of those who lost and those who, in some cases, had to leave their homes and hopes behind has receded from public discourse. Yet the debates about what was achieved continue to matter, as do those about whether further decolonization—of cultures, of economic relationships, of languages—in the international arena is necessary, or whether subsequent disappointments suggest instead that the reality and the hopes of decolonization were misconceived from the start. In these and other ways, the era and the promise of decolonization continue to shape our world.

NOTES

[1] Brian MacArthur, ed., *Penguin Book of Twentieth-Century Speeches* (London: Penguin Viking, 1992), 234–37.

[2] "Report: First Day of Independence," 8pm News, Radiotélévision française (RTF).

[3] Todd Shepard, *The Invention of Decolonization: The Algerian War and the Remaking of France*, 2nd ed. (Ithaca, N.Y.: Cornell University Press, 2008), 5.

[4] Abdoulaye Ly, *Les masses africaines et l'actuelle condition humaine* (Paris: Présence africaine, 1956), 12; Georges Balandier, introduction to Alfred Sauvy, ed., *Le "tiers-monde": Sous-développement et développement* (Paris: INDED, 1956), 13.

[5] Shepard, *The Invention of Decolonization*, 68.

[6] Frank Heinlein, *British Government Policy and Decolonisation, 1945–1963: Scrutinising the Official Mind* (London: Routledge, 2002), 88.

[7] Winston S. Churchill, *India* (London: Thornton Butterworth, 1931), 94.

[8] "Memorial Day Brings Hopes of a Better Post-war World," *Life*, June 15, 1942, 36–37.

[9] Samuel Rosenman, ed., *The Public Papers and Addresses of Franklin D. Roosevelt* (New York: Random House, 1950), 10:314.

[10] Jawaharlal Nehru, *The Discovery of India* (Calcutta: Signet Press, 1948), 426.

[11] Vladimir I. Lenin, *Imperialism: The Highest Stage of Capitalism* (1917).

[12] H. L. Wesseling, "Post-Colonial Holland," *Journal of Contemporary History* 15, no. 1 (January 1980): 126.

[13] Benedetto Croce, *Contro l'approvazione del dettato della pace* (Bari: Laterza, 1947), 8–9.

[14] *Chronology of International Events and Documents* 2, no. 2 (January 1946): 47; Stephen Howe, *Anticolonialism in British Politics: The Left and the End of Empire, 1918–1964* (Oxford: Clarendon Press, 1993), 144.

[15] Germaine Tillion, *L'Algérie en 57* (Paris: Les Éditions de Minuit, 1957), 28.

[16] Gyanendra Pandey, *Remembering Partition: Violence, Nationalism and History in India* (Cambridge: Cambridge University Press, 2002), 67–91.

[17] Claude Bourdet, "Votre gestapo d'Algérie," *France-Observateur*, January 13, 1955, 6–7.

[18] Martin Meredith, *Mandela: A Biography* (New York: Public Affairs, 2011), 129.

PART TWO

The Documents

1

1945–1947:
Decolonization Becomes Imaginable

1

WINSTON CHURCHILL

"Hands Off the British Empire"

December 31, 1944

In the fall of 1944, as World War II began to draw to a close, U.S. secretary of state Cordell Hull forwarded a memorandum to the British government concerning the future of Southeast Asia. It suggested that all of the Allies with imperial interests in the region—the United States in the Philippines, the Dutch in the Dutch East Indies (present-day Indonesia), the French in Indochina (Vietnam, Laos, and Cambodia), and the British in their Malay Peninsula and island dependencies of Malaysia and Singapore—should make a joint declaration. Ideally, this would include, "1) specific dates when independence or complete (dominion) self-government will be accorded, 2) specific steps to be taken to develop native capacity for self-rule, and 3) a pledge of economic autonomy and equality of economic treatment toward other nations."[1] British prime minister Winston Churchill sent the following telegram to his foreign secretary, Anthony Eden, whom Churchill had dispatched to Washington for discussions. It refers specifically to the Hull memo while capturing the prime minister's attachment to the empire and his assessment of critics of British colonial rule.

---

[1] Cordell Hull, *The Memoirs of Cordell Hull*, vol. 2 (New York: Macmillan, 1948), 1600.

From Akira Iriye, *The Cold War in Asia: A Historical Introduction* (Englewood Cliffs, N.J.: Prentice-Hall, 1974), 87.

There must be no question of our being hustled or seduced into declarations affecting British sovereignty in any of the Dominions or Colonies. Pray remember my declaration against liquidating the British Empire. If the Americans want to take Japanese islands which they have conquered, let them do so with our blessing and any form of words that may be agreeable to them. But "hands off the British Empire" is our maxim and it must not be weakened or smirched to please sob-stuff merchants at home or foreigners of any hue.

2

UNITED NATIONS

United Nations Charter: Preamble and Declaration concerning Non-autonomous Territories

June 26, 1945

After World War I, U.S. president Woodrow Wilson succeeded in establishing the League of Nations, an international body where representatives of sovereign states could address issues of the day, ongoing disputes, and projects for the future. The league was widely judged to be a failure, however. The United States did not participate (Congress blocked the treaty), the new Soviet Union was not permitted to join, and the organization proved incapable of either making decisions or enforcing those decisions it did make. When, for example, Italy invaded Ethiopia in 1935 and colonized the only African state that had never previously suffered European rule, the league did little.

Still, the idea of a more effective international body survived the beginning of World War II. In 1941, Britain and the United States issued the Atlantic Charter, a policy statement that defined the Allies' goals for the postwar world. To amplify the moral need for victory against the Axis Powers that the Atlantic Charter affirmed, all of the major Allies signed the January 1, 1942, Declaration of the United Nations. In secret negotiations, representatives from China, Great Britain, the USSR, and the

From United Nations Charter, San Francisco, June 26, 1945, www.un.org/en /documents/charter/.

United States planned how the UN would work. Their so-called Dumbarton Oaks proposal (named after the estate in Washington, D.C., where it was elaborated) became the subject of widespread discussion within Allied countries. These debates shaped what became the United Nations Charter, which in March 1945 all countries that had declared war on the defeated Axis Powers were invited to sign.

The following excerpts from the charter are taken from the preamble, which makes big and inspiring claims about the organization's goals, and the articles, which read like legal treaties and are more limited in scope. South African prime minister Jan Smuts, a firm believer in both the separation of the "races" and the British Empire, authored the preamble. Note that the affirmation of a principle of national self-determination, which had made Wilson's "Fourteen Points" speech of 1918 (in which he first called for the League of Nations) and the Atlantic Charter such rallying cries for anticolonialists, is absent from the document.

Preamble

WE THE PEOPLES OF THE UNITED NATIONS DETERMINED

- to save succeeding generations from the scourge of war, which twice in our lifetime has brought untold sorrow to mankind, and
- to reaffirm faith in fundamental human rights, in the dignity and worth of the human person, in the equal rights of men and women and of nations large and small, and
- to establish conditions under which justice and respect for the obligations arising from treaties and other sources of international law can be maintained, and
- to promote social progress and better standards of life in larger freedom,

AND FOR THESE ENDS

- to practice tolerance and live together in peace with one another as good neighbours, and
- to unite our strength to maintain international peace and security, and

- to ensure, by the acceptance of principles and the institution of methods, that armed force shall not be used, save in the common interest, and
- to employ international machinery for the promotion of the economic and social advancement of all peoples,

HAVE RESOLVED TO COMBINE OUR EFFORTS TO ACCOMPLISH THESE AIMS

Accordingly, our respective Governments, through representatives assembled in the city of San Francisco, who have exhibited their full powers found to be in good and due form, have agreed to the present Charter of the United Nations and do hereby establish an international organization to be known as the United Nations. . . .

Chapter XI

ARTICLE 73

Members of the United Nations which have or assume responsibilities for the administration of territories whose peoples have not yet attained a full measure of self-government recognize the principle that the interests of the inhabitants of these territories are paramount, and accept as a sacred trust the obligation to promote to the utmost, within the system of international peace and security established by the present Charter, the well-being of the inhabitants of these territories, and, to this end:

a. to ensure, with due respect for the culture of the peoples concerned, their political, economic, social, and educational advancement, their just treatment, and their protection against abuses;

b. to develop self-government, to take due account of the political aspirations of the peoples, and to assist them in the progressive development of their free political institutions, according to the particular circumstances of each territory and its peoples and their varying stages of advancement;

c. to further international peace and security;

d. to promote constructive measures of development, to encourage research, and to co-operate with one another and, when and where appropriate, with specialized international bodies with a view to the practical achievement of the social, economic, and scientific purposes set forth in this Article; and

e. to transmit regularly to the Secretary-General for information purposes, subject to such limitation as security and constitutional considerations may require, statistical and other information of a technical nature relating to economic, social, and educational conditions in the territories for which they are respectively responsible other than those territories to which Chapters XII and XIII apply.

ARTICLE 74

Members of the United Nations also agree that their policy in respect of the territories to which this Chapter applies, no less than in respect of their metropolitan areas, must be based on the general principle of good-neighbourliness, due account being taken of the interests and well-being of the rest of the world, in social, economic, and commercial matters.

3

HO CHI MINH

Declaration of Independence of the Democratic Republic of Vietnam
September 2, 1945

In 1941, the leader of the Communist party of Vietnam proposed that all groups involved in resisting the Japanese occupation form a united front, which took the name League for the Independence of Vietnam (Vietnam Doc Lap Dong Minh Hoi). It was usually referred to as the Viet Minh League. Nguyen Sinh Cung, better known by his nom de guerre, Ho Chi Minh, soon came to lead this organization. By the end of World War II, the Viet Minh League had gained control over large parts of northern Vietnam, where it began to establish local governments and oversee the redistribution of land to peasant farmers. On September 2, 1945, Ho Chi Minh read the following declaration in Ba Dinh Square, in the colonial

From Ho Chi Minh, *Selected Works* (Hanoi: Foreign Languages Publishing House, 1961), 3:17–21.

capital of Hanoi (see Map 3, page 11). Tens of thousands of people wit-
nessed this act, yet the text itself also spoke directly to audiences far from
Hanoi (see Document 4).

All men are created equal. They are endowed by their Creator with certain inalienable rights, among these are Life, Liberty and the pursuit of
Happiness.

This immortal statement was made in the Declaration of Independence of the United States of America in 1776. In a broader sense, this
means: All the peoples on the earth are equal from birth, all the peoples
have a right to live, to be happy and free.

The Declaration of the French Revolution made in 1791 on the Rights
of Man and the Citizen also states: "Men are born and remain free and
equal in rights."

Those are undeniable truths.

Nevertheless, for more than eighty years, the French imperialists,
abusing the standard of Liberty, Equality, and Fraternity, have violated
our Fatherland and oppressed our fellow-citizens. They have acted contrary to the ideals of humanity and justice.

In the field of politics, they have deprived our people of every democratic liberty.

They have enforced inhuman laws; they have set up three distinct
political regimes in the North, the Center and the South of Vietnam in
order to wreck our national unity and prevent our people from being
united.

They have built more prisons than schools. They have mercilessly
slain our patriots; they have drowned our uprisings in rivers of blood.

They have fettered public opinion; they have fostered ignorance
among our people.

To weaken our race they have forced us to use opium and alcohol.

In the field of economics, they have fleeced us to the backbone,
impoverished our people, and devastated our land.

They have robbed us of our rice fields, our mines, our forests, and
our raw materials. They have monopolized the issuing of bank-notes
and the export trade.

They have invented numerous unjustifiable taxes and reduced our
people, especially our peasantry, to a state of extreme poverty.

They have hampered the prospering of our national bourgeoisie;
they have mercilessly exploited our workers.

In the autumn of 1940, when the Japanese Fascists violated Indochina's territory to establish new bases in their fight against the Allies, the French imperialists went down on their bended knees and handed over our country to them.

Thus, from that date, our people were subjected to the double yoke of the French and the Japanese. Their sufferings and miseries increased. The result was that from the end of last year to the beginning of this year, from Quang Tri province to the North of Vietnam, more than two million of our fellow-citizens died from starvation. On March 9, the French troops were disarmed by the Japanese. The French colonialists either fled or surrendered showing that not only were they incapable of "protecting" us, but that, in the span of five years, they had twice sold our country to the Japanese.

On several occasions before March 9, the Viet Minh League urged the French to ally themselves with it against the Japanese. Instead of agreeing to this proposal, the French colonialists so intensified their terrorist activities against the Viet Minh members that before fleeing they massacred a great number of our political prisoners detained at Yen Bay and Cao Bang.

Notwithstanding all this, our fellow-citizens have always manifested toward the French a tolerant and humane attitude. Even after the Japanese putsch of March 1945, the Viet Minh League helped many Frenchmen to cross the frontier, rescued some of them from Japanese jails, and protected French lives and property.

From the autumn of 1940, our country had in fact ceased to be a French colony and had become a Japanese possession.

After the Japanese had surrendered to the Allies, our whole people rose to regain our national sovereignty and to found the Democratic Republic of Vietnam.

The truth is that we have wrested our independence from the Japanese and not from the French.

The French have fled, the Japanese have capitulated, Emperor Bao Dai has abdicated. Our people have broken the chains which for nearly a century have fettered them and have won independence for the Fatherland. Our people at the same time have overthrown the monarchic regime that has reigned supreme for dozens of centuries. In its place has been established the present Democratic Republic.

For these reasons, we, members of the Provisional Government, representing the whole Vietnamese people, declare that from now on we break off all relations of a colonial character with France; we repeal all the international obligation that France has so far subscribed to on behalf of Vietnam and we abolish all the special rights the French have unlawfully acquired in our Fatherland.

The whole Vietnamese people, animated by a common purpose, are determined to fight to the bitter end against any attempt by the French colonialists to reconquer their country.

We are convinced that the Allied nations which at [the 1943 "Big Three" meeting between Joseph Stalin, Winston Churchill, and Franklin Roosevelt in] Tehran and [in signing the 1945 United Nations Charter in] San Francisco have acknowledged the principles of self-determination and equality of nations, will not refuse to acknowledge the independence of Vietnam.

A people who have courageously opposed French domination for more than eight years, a people who have fought side by side with the Allies against the Fascists during these last years, such a people must be free and independent.

For these reasons, we, members of the Provisional Government of the Democratic Republic of Vietnam, solemnly declare to the world that Vietnam has the right to be a free and independent country—and in fact is so already. The entire Vietnamese people are determined to mobilize all their physical and mental strength, to sacrifice their lives and property in order to safeguard their independence and liberty.

4

An Appeal of the Vietnamese Bishops in Favor of the Independence of Their Country

September 23, 1945

On September 23, 1945, soon after Ho Chi Minh proclaimed Vietnamese independence in Hanoi (see Document 3), four Roman Catholic bishops of Vietnamese origin put their names on this public letter to Pope Pius XII. On November 4, 1945, as French troops moved to reassert control over their nation's Southeast Asian colonies, the same men published the "Message of the Four Vietnamese Bishops to the Christians of the World and to the People of the United States of America and the United

From *Bulletin des missions*, January–March 1946, 38–40. Translation by author.

Kingdom." In both instances, the Viet Minh League leadership asked the bishops to intervene, the appeals were broadcast by the new Democratic Republic of Vietnam state radio, and the state and its allies abroad published copies and distributed them internationally. Copies were left on the steps of some churches in Paris as well. The bishops spoke for the 1.2 million Catholics in Vietnam at the time. Catholicism had been brought to the region by missionaries in an effort long supported by European colonial powers.

Our beloved people of Vietnam have sought to take advantage of the mediation of their four bishops to extend the honor of their deep respect for Your Holiness and to implore Your benediction, your magnanimity and prayers in favor of our independence, which it has just acquired and intends to hold on to whatever the cost.

Our Government has taken the happy and thoughtful decision to adopt as Vietnam's national holiday the holiday that the Holy See [the Vatican] authorized for our Vietnamese martyrs, the first Sunday of September. All Vietnamese people, regardless of their religion, will celebrate this festival of September 2nd in a spirit of unprecedented and sincere patriotism, through grandiose and enthusiastic events, which will give witness to their shared and unshakable resolve to defend their government until death.

In the face of these extremely moving events, and touched to the depths of our hearts by the sacred trust we owe our Fatherland, we the Vietnamese bishops implore Your Holiness, the court in Rome, their eminences the cardinals, their excellencies the archbishops, the bishops, and all of the world's Catholics, especially of France, to support the decision of our cherished nation. With deep veneration and filial devotion.

2

Defining New International Connections

5

FIFTH PAN-AFRICAN CONGRESS

The Challenge to the Colonial Powers

1945

In 1919, the first Pan-African Congress met in Paris, concomitant with the Paris Peace Conference negotiations that followed World War I. The American writer and activist W. E. B. DuBois organized the meeting, and the French deputy from the Senegalese city of Dakar, Blaise Diagne, presided. The fifth Pan-African Congress, which met at the close of World War II in Manchester, England, was the first such gathering to be dominated by delegates from Africa. Its primary organizer was George Padmore, a Trinidadian radical activist who, after he left the Communist party in the 1930s, had focused on Pan-African politics (which, in his view, should build on the shared struggles of all people with roots in sub-Saharan Africa). Younger West Africans, notably the Sierra Leonean labor activist Wallace Johnson and Kwame Nkrumah, from the Gold Coast (now Ghana), also played key roles and helped focus attention on Africa itself. While questions of racism and economic injustice remained important, delegates to the congress gave priority to the need to end colonialism. In the following document, notice the way they explain the roots of their current concerns, the extent and limits of their demands, and the different means they propose to achieve them.

From George Padmore, *Pan-Africanism or Communism: The Coming Struggle for Africa* (New York: Roy Publishers, 1956), 170.

The delegates to the Fifth Pan-African Congress believe in peace. How could it be otherwise when for centuries the African peoples have been victims of violence and slavery. Yet if the Western world is still determined to rule mankind by force, then Africans, as a last resort, may have to appeal to force in the effort to achieve Freedom, even if force destroys them and the world.

We are determined to be free. We want education. We want the right to earn a decent living; the right to express our thoughts and emotions, to adopt and create forms of beauty. We demand for Black Africa autonomy and independence, so far and no further than it is possible in this "One World" for groups and peoples to rule themselves subject to inevitable world unity and federation.

We are not ashamed to have been an age-long patient people. We continue willingly to sacrifice and strive. But we are unwilling to starve any longer while doing the world's drudgery, in order to support by our poverty and ignorance a false aristocracy and a discarded imperialism.

We condemn the monopoly of capital and the rule of private wealth and industry for private profit alone. We welcome economic democracy as the only real democracy. Therefore, we shall complain, appeal and arraign. We will make the world listen to the facts of our condition. We will fight in every way we can for freedom, democracy and social betterment.

6

UNESCO

The Statement on Race

July 1950

In addition to questions of political sovereignty, debates around racism and its role in colonialism influenced all episodes of decolonization in the years after World War II. In 1949, some one hundred scientists and social scientists were called together under the auspices of the United Nations Educational, Scientific, and Cultural Organization (UNESCO),

From UNESCO, *Four Statements on the Race Question* (Paris: UNESCO, 1969), 30, 32–35.

with the goal of synthesizing a clear statement about the science of "race" that could shape public discussions. In this task, they received advice and assistance from diplomats, politicians, and bureaucrats associated with UNESCO. Their statement, published in 1950, was clear in its rejection of many previous presumptions about the concept of race, and almost immediately it sparked substantial controversy, on both political and scientific grounds.

Less than a year after its publication, UNESCO published a revised version of the statement, which included more input from biologists and physical anthropologists. The original 1950 version, however, had far more popular impact and is excerpted here. Note the role that scientific authority plays in its claims. Consider also the tension in the text between asserting respect for differences among various groups and making claims of sameness. Interestingly, the entire text is structured as a point-by-point (though tacit) rebuttal of Adolf Hitler's book Mein Kampf *(My Struggle).*

1. Scientists have reached general agreement in recognising that mankind is one: that all men belong to the same species, *homo sapiens*. It is further generally agreed among scientists that all men are probably derived from the same common stock; and that such differences as exist between different groups of mankind are due to the operation of evolutionary factors of differentiation such as isolation, the drift and random fixation of the material particles which control heredity (the genes), changes in the structure of these particles, hybridisation, and natural selection. In these ways groups have arisen of varying stability and degree of differentiation which have been classified in different ways for different purposes.

2. From the biological standpoint, the species *homo sapiens* is made up of a number of populations, each one of which differs from the others in the frequency of one or more genes. Such genes, responsible for the hereditary differences between men, are always few when compared to the whole genetic constitution of man and to the vast number of genes common to all human beings regardless of the population to which they belong. This means that the likenesses among men are far greater than their differences.

. . .

10. The scientific material available to us at present does not justify the conclusion that inherited genetic differences are a major factor in

producing the differences between the cultures and cultural achievements of different peoples or groups. It does indicate, however, that
the history of the cultural experience which each group has undergone
is the major factor in explaining such differences. The one trait which
above all others has been at a premium in the evolution of men's mental characters [characteristics] has been educability, plasticity. This is a
trait which all human beings possess. It is indeed, a species character
of *homo sapiens*.

11. So far as temperament is concerned, there is no definite evidence
that there exist inborn differences between human groups. There is evidence that whatever group differences of the kind there might be are
greatly overridden by the individual differences, and by the differences
springing from environmental factors.

12. As for personality and character, these may be considered race-
less. In every human group a rich variety of personality and character
types will be found, and there is no reason for believing that any human
group is richer than any other in these respects.

13. With respect to race mixture, the evidence points unequivo-
cally to the fact that this has been going on from the earliest times.
Indeed, one of the chief processes of race formation and race extinc-
tion or absorption is by means of hybridisation between races or ethnic
groups. Furthermore, no convincing evidence has been adduced that
race mixture of itself produces biologically bad effects. Statements that
human hybrids frequently show undesirable traits, both physically and
mentally, physical disharmonies and mental degeneracies, are not supported by the facts. There is, therefore, no biological justification for
prohibiting intermarriage between persons of different ethnic groups.

14. The biological fact of race and the myth of "race" should be distinguished. For all practical social purposes "race" is not so much a biological phenomenon as a social myth. The myth of "race" has created an
enormous amount of human and social damage. In recent years it has
taken a heavy toll in human lives and caused untold suffering. It still prevents the normal development of millions of human beings and deprives
civilisation of the effective co-operation of productive minds. The biological differences between ethnic groups should be disregarded from
the standpoint of social acceptance and social action. The unity of mankind from both the biological and social viewpoints is the main thing. To
recognise this and to act accordingly is the first requirement of modern
man. It is but to recognise what a great biologist wrote in 1875: "As
man advances in civilisation, and small tribes are united into larger communities, the simplest reason would tell each individual that he ought

to extend his social instincts and sympathies to all the members of the same nation, though personally unknown to him. This point being once reached, there is only an artificial barrier to prevent his sympathies extending to the men of all nations and races." These are the words of Charles Darwin in *The Descent of Man* (2nd ed., 1875, pp. 187–8). And, indeed, the whole of human history shows that a co-operative spirit is not only natural to men, but more deeply rooted than any self-seeking tendencies. If this were not so we should not see the growth of integration and organisation of his communities which the centuries and the millenniums plainly exhibit.

15. We now have to consider the bearing of these statements on the problem of human equality. It must be asserted with the utmost emphasis that equality as an ethical principle in no way depends upon the assertion that human beings are in fact equal in endowment. Obviously individuals in all ethnic groups vary greatly among themselves in endowment. Nevertheless, the characteristics in which human groups differ from one another are often exaggerated and used as a basis for questioning the validity of equality in the ethical sense. For this purpose we have thought it worthwhile to set out in a formal manner what is at present scientifically established concerning individual and group differences.

a. In matters of race, the only characteristics which anthropologists can effectively use as a basis for classifications are physical and physiological.

b. According to present knowledge there is no proof that the groups of mankind differ in their innate mental characteristics, whether in respect of intelligence or temperament. The scientific evidence indicates that the range of mental capacities in all ethnic groups is much the same.

c. Historical and sociological studies support the view that genetic differences are not of importance in determining the social and cultural differences between different groups of *Homo sapiens*, and that the social and cultural changes in different groups have, in the main, been independent of changes in inborn constitution. Vast social changes have occurred which were not in any way connected with changes in racial type.

d. There is no evidence that race mixture as such produces bad results from the biological point of view. The social results of race mixture whether for good or ill are to be traced to social factors.

e. All normal human beings are capable of learning to share in a common life, to understand the nature of mutual service and reciprocity, and to respect social obligations and contracts. Such biological differences as exist between members of different ethnic groups have no relevance to problems of social and political organisation, moral life and communication between human beings.

Lastly, biological studies lend support to the ethic of universal brotherhood; for man is born with drives toward co-operation, and unless these drives are satisfied, men and nations alike fall ill. Man is born a social being who can reach his fullest development only through interaction with his fellows. The denial at any point of this social bond between men and man brings with it disintegration. In this sense, every man is his brother's keeper. For every man is a piece of the continent, a part of the main, because he is involved in mankind.

Original statement drafted at UNESCO House, Paris, by the following experts:

Prof. Ernest Beaglehole (New Zealand);
Professor Juan Comas (Mexico);
Professor L. A. Costa Pinto (Brazil);
Professor Franklin Frazier (United States of America);
Professor Morris Ginsberg (United Kingdom);
Dr. Humayun Kabir (India);
Professor Claude Lévi-Strauss (France);
Professor Ashley Montagu (United States of America) *(rapporteur)*.

Text revised by Professor Ashley Montagu, after criticism submitted by Professors Hadley Cantril, E. G. Conklin, Gunnar Dahlberg, Theodosius Dobzhansky, L. C. Dunn, Donald Hager, Julian S. Huxley, Otto Klineberg, Wilbert Moore, H. J. Muller, Gunnar Myrdal, Joseph Needham, Curt Stern.

7

ALFRED SAUVY

Three Worlds, One Planet

August 14, 1952

Alfred Sauvy was an influential French demographer (an expert on the growth and decline of human populations) who published the first text to introduce the term third world *into international discussions about global relations. His article appeared in the* Observateur *(Observer), a left-wing French magazine known for its criticism of both the Soviet Union and the United States. In the following excerpts, he combines a political analysis of the cold war, which brought into conflict the "first" (Western, or pro-U.S.) and "second" (Eastern, or pro-Soviet) worlds, and a social scientific argument about how population growth would trump political projects. It was only the final lines, however, that became widely cited, in which Sauvy adroitly compares the third world to the Third Estate. In pre-revolutionary France, the Third Estate was a legal category that included well over 90 percent of the population, in contrast to the much smaller First Estate (clergy) and Second Estate (aristocracy). The common people of the Third Estate produced most of France's wealth, but they played no direct role in how the country was governed. According to many interpretations, the disregard and exploitation of the Third Estate caused the French Revolution of 1789.*

We readily speak of the existence of two worlds, of the possibility of war between them, of their coexistence, yet all too often we forget that a third world also exists, the most important of all and, really, in terms of chronological age, the first world. It consists of all those countries that, in United Nations–speak, are called underdeveloped.

Things appear differently when we take the point of view of this largest group: From their perspective, two vanguards are several centuries ahead, the Western and the Eastern. Is it necessary to follow one or the other, or is a different path possible?

From Alfred Sauvy, "Trois mondes, une planète," *L'Observateur*, August 14, 1952, 14. Translation by author.

Without the third—or maybe the first—world, the coexistence of the other two would not pose a big problem. . . .

What interests each of the two [developed] worlds is to conquer the third, or at least to have it on its side. And this is what makes coexistence so difficult. . . .

Unfortunately, the struggle to control the third world does not permit the other two to go peacefully along their way, each one in its separate valley, the best one, of course, the only one, the "true path." . . .

[Both sides are fixated on the other, but this fixation prevents each from recognizing the enormous pressure for dramatic changes that is coming from the third world.]

The underdeveloped countries, the third world, have entered a new stage. Certain medical techniques are becoming widespread for one important reason: They cost so little. A whole region of Algeria was cleansed of malaria by DDT: It cost 68 francs [a few dollars] a person. Elsewhere, in Ceylon, in India, etc., similar results have been achieved. For a few cents, a man's life span grows by several years. Thanks to this, those countries have the [low] mortality rates we achieved by 1914 but still have the [high] birthrates we had in the eighteenth century. Certainly, economic conditions improve: a lower child mortality rate, a higher rate of productivity among adults, etc. Yet still it is easy to grasp that this demographic growth needs to be accompanied by substantial investments so that these societies can meet the needs of their inhabitants. But these necessary investments cost much more than 68 francs a person. The financial needs of the cold war make it impossible for these other needs to be met. Can you not hear, on the French Riviera, the voices crying out across the Mediterranean, from Egypt or from Tunisia? Do you think what is happening there is nothing more than palace intrigues or the gesticulations of a few ambitious men, eager to push into power? No, no: The pressure is rising steadily in the boiler room of humanity.

For all the misery of today, for all of tomorrow's catastrophes, there is one untouchable remedy. You know what it is: It drips slowly on our side from the demands of the Atlantic pact [which created the North Atlantic Treaty Organization, or NATO] and on the other side from the agitated production of weapons that will no longer be up-to-date in three years' time.

There's a mathematically certain outcome to this brinkmanship. . . . Since preparations for war are the first concern, secondary cares such as world hunger require only enough attention to avoid an explosion, or more accurately, only enough to allow the first objective to carry on unimpeded. Yet when one thinks about how, in every era, conservatives have failed to correctly measure the limits of human patience, it saps any confidence one might have in the Americans' ability to master the heat boiling up among the world's peoples. Neophytes of domination, so enchanted with free enterprise that they understand it as an end in itself, they have clearly not taken note that underdeveloped countries of the feudal type can slide much more easily into a Communist regime than into democratic capitalism. It might console us, if we want, to see this as clear proof that capitalism has gone much farther down the road, but the fact remains the same. And should it cast its bright glow over the first world, perhaps the latter, even if any reaction of human solidarity were absent, might begin to recognize a slow and irresistible thrust, humble and fierce, toward life. Because that third world, ignored, exploited, and despised, like the Third Estate, wants to be something, too.

8

FIRST AFRO-ASIAN CONFERENCE

Final Communiqué

April 24, 1955

In 1955, the first Afro-Asian Conference, known as the Bandung Conference for the city in which it was held, brought together the leaders of twenty-nine countries in the recently independent Republic of Indonesia (see Map 3, page 11). The man who had led his country's violent struggle against the Dutch, Ahmed Sukarno, invited leaders of recently decolonized independent states, such as India, the Philippines, and Pakistan, as well as representatives of states that had recently cast off Western domination, notably the People's Republic of China and Egypt, to discuss what united them and how they could influence world events. The conference also welcomed leaders and representatives of groups fighting for independence and against colonialism. The Algerian National Liberation Front (FLN), in particular, garnered enormous attention and support at Bandung.

From *Foreign Policy of India: Texts of Documents, 1947–64* (New Delhi: Lok Sabha Secretariat, 1966), 525–31.

The Final Communiqué of the conference was remarkable for its forthright and critical assessment of the history and continuing existence of Western overseas colonialism. Diplomatic formulas did little to soften the verbal blows. While economic cooperation was a key element of the document, the following excerpts highlight the areas that received the most attention at the time—for example, the continuing effects of colonial rule in the Arab world and in Africa, particularly North Africa.

The Asian-African Conference, convened upon the invitation of the Prime Ministers of Burma, Ceylon, India, Indonesia and Pakistan, met in Bandung from the 18th to the 24th April, 1955. In addition to the sponsoring countries the following 24 countries participated in the Conference:

1. Afghanistan
2. Cambodia
3. People's Republic of China
4. Egypt
5. Ethiopia
6. Gold Coast
7. Iran
8. Iraq
9. Japan
10. Jordan
11. Laos
12. Lebanon
13. Liberia
14. Libya
15. Nepal
16. Philippines
17. Saudi Arabia
18. Sudan
19. Syria
20. Thailand
21. Turkey

22. Democratic Republic of Vietnam

23. State of Vietnam

24. Yemen

The Asian-African Conference considered problems of common interest and concern to countries of Asia and Africa and discussed ways and means by which their people could achieve fuller economic, cultural and political cooperation. . . .

Cultural Cooperation

1. The Asian-African Conference was convinced that among the most powerful means of promoting understanding among nations is the development of cultural cooperation. Asia and Africa have been the cradle of great religions and civilizations, which have enriched other cultures and civilizations while themselves being enriched in the process. Thus the cultures of Asia and Africa are based on spiritual and universal foundations. Unfortunately contacts among Asian and African countries were interrupted during the past centuries. The peoples of Asia and Africa are now animated by a keen and sincere desire to renew their old cultural contacts and develop new ones in the context of the modern world. All participating Governments at the Conference reiterated their determination to work for closer cultural cooperation.

2. The Asian-African Conference took note of the fact that the existence of colonialism in many parts of Asia and Africa, in whatever form it may be, not only prevents cultural cooperation but also suppresses the national cultures of the people. Some colonial powers have denied to their dependent peoples basic rights in the sphere of education and culture, which hampers the development of their personality and also prevents cultural intercourse with other Asian and African peoples. This is particularly true in the case of Tunisia, Algeria and Morocco, where the basic right of the people to study their own language and culture has been suppressed. Similar discrimination has been practiced against African and coloured people in some parts of the Continent of Africa. The Conference felt that these policies amount to a denial of the fundamental rights of man, impede cultural advancement in this region and also hamper cultural cooperation on the wider international plane. The Conference condemned such a denial of fundamental rights in the sphere of education and culture in some parts of Asia and Africa by this and other forms of cultural suppression. In particular, the Conference condemned racialism as a means of cultural suppression.

3. It was not from any sense of exclusiveness or rivalry with other groups of nations and other civilizations and cultures that the Conference viewed the development of cultural cooperation among Asian and African countries. True to the age-old tradition of tolerance and universality, the Conference believed that Asian and African cultural cooperation should be developed in the larger context of world cooperation.

Side by side with the development of Asian-African cultural cooperation the countries of Asia and Africa desire to develop cultural contacts with others. This would enrich their own culture and would also help in the promotion of world peace and understanding. . . .

Human Rights and Self-Determination

1. The Asian-African Conference declared its full support of the fundamental principles of Human Rights as set forth in the Charter of the United Nations and took note of the Universal Declaration of Human Rights as a common standard of achievement for all peoples and all nations. The Conference declared its full support of the principle of self-determination of peoples and nations as set forth in the Charter of the United Nations and took note of the United Nations resolutions on the rights of peoples and nations to self-determination, which is a prerequisite of the full enjoyment of all fundamental Human Rights.

2. The Asian-African Conference deplored the policies and practices of racial segregation and discrimination, which form the basis of government and human relations in large regions of Africa and in other parts of the world. Such conduct is not only a gross violation of human rights, but also a denial of the dignity of man. The Conference extended its warm sympathy and support for the courageous stand taken by the victims of racial discrimination, especially by the peoples of African and Indian and Pakistani origin in South Africa; applauded all those who sustain their cause; reaffirmed the determination of Asian-African peoples to eradicate every trace of racialism that might exist in their own countries; and pledged to use its full moral influence to guard against the danger of falling victims to the same evil in their struggle to eradicate it.

Problems of Dependent Peoples

1. The Asian-African Conference discussed the problems of dependent peoples and colonialism and the evils arising from the subjection of peoples to alien subjugation and exploitation. The Conference is agreed:

a. In declaring that colonialism in all its manifestations is an evil which should speedily be brought to an end;

b. In affirming that the subjection of peoples to alien subjugation, domination and exploitation constitutes a denial of fundamental human rights, is contrary to the Charter of the United Nations and is an impediment to the promotion of world peace and cooperation;

c. In declaring its support of the cause of freedom and independence for all such peoples, and

d. In calling upon the powers concerned to grant freedom and independence to such peoples.

2. In view of the unsettled situation in North Africa and of the persisting denial to the peoples of North Africa of their right to self-determination, the Asian-African Conference declared its support of the rights of the people of Algeria, Morocco and Tunisia to self-determination and independence and urged the French Government to bring about a peaceful settlement of the issue without delay.

Other Problems

1. In view of the existing tension in the Middle East, caused by the situation in Palestine and of the danger of that tension to world peace, the Asian-African Conference declared its support of the rights of the Arab people of Palestine and called for the implementation of the United Nations Resolutions on Palestine and the achievement of the peaceful settlement of the Palestine question. . . .

. . . The Asian-African Conference recommended that the Five Sponsoring Countries consider the convening of the next meeting of the Conference, in consultation with the participating countries.

BANDUNG, 24 April, 1955

9

RICHARD WRIGHT

The Color Curtain: A Report on the Bandung Conference

1956

The African American writer Richard Wright was one of the many independent observers who went to Indonesia to cover the Bandung Conference of 1955 (see Document 8). In The Color Curtain, *published shortly after the conference, Wright reported on this unprecedented gathering of anticolonial leaders. In Bandung, as he famously wrote, "the despised, the insulted, the hurt, the dispossessed . . . the underdogs of the human race were meeting." The conference gave the so-called third world a voice and a face and set the stage for the emergence of a group that called itself the Non-Aligned Movement. While many of the states in attendance were firmly on one side or the other of the U.S.-Soviet cold war, states such as India, Indonesia, and Egypt were actively looking to formulate their own approach to world politics. Several years later, when the Chinese Communist government broke with the Soviet Union, the idea that it might be possible to avoid alignment received new impetus. Still, many observers viewed nonalignment as more threatening to the West than to the Soviets and their allies.*

Wright, who had come to international prominence with the publication of his controversial novel Native Son *in 1940, left the United States for France in 1949. His decision to go into exile was driven by his anger at both the racist climate he saw in his homeland and the Communist Party of the United States (CPUSA). A former member of the party, he quit partly because he believed that it, among other flaws, neither took racism seriously nor understood how racism shaped politics. Wright went to Bandung with much excitement, hoping to see how other people of color were charting their own paths. As this excerpt reveals, however, he left with more-mixed feelings. In particular, as the last line suggests, he warned of the attraction that communism might have for anticolonialists if the West ignored them, a temptation he embodies in the person of Chinese prime minister Zhou Enlai.*

From Richard Wright, *Black Power: Three Books from Exile* (New York: Harper Perennial, 2008), 540–42, 593.

At last Sukarno, President of the Republic of Indonesia, mounted the rostrum to deliver the opening address. . . .

He was a small man, tan of face, and with a pair of dark, deep-set eyes; he moved slowly, deliberately. He spoke in English with a slight accent; he knew words and how to use them, and you realized at once that this man had done nothing all his life but utilize words to capture the attention and loyalties of others. From the very outset, he sounded the notes of race and religion, strong, defiant; before he had uttered more than a hundred syllables, he declared:

"This is the first international conference of colored peoples in the history of mankind!" . . .

And why had they now come together? Sukarno said:

". . . We are living in a world of fear. The life of man today is corroded and made bitter by fear. Fear of the future, fear of the hydrogen bomb, fear of ideologies. Perhaps this fear is a greater danger than the danger itself, because it is fear which drives men to act foolishly, to act thoughtlessly, to act dangerously. . . . And do not think that the oceans and the seas will protect us. The food we eat, the water that we drink, yes, even the very air that we breathe can be contaminated by poisons originating from thousands of miles away. And it could be that, even if we ourselves escaped lightly, the unborn generations of our children would bear on their distorted bodies the marks of our failure to control the forces which have been released on the world."

What strength had Sukarno and Asian and African leaders like him? He was frank about it. He said:

"For many generations our peoples have been the voiceless ones in the world. We have been the unregarded, the peoples for whom decisions were made by others whose interests were paramount, the peoples who lived in poverty and humiliation. . . . What can we do? The peoples of Asia and Africa wield little physical power. Even our economic strength is dispersed and slight. We cannot indulge in power politics. . . . Our statesmen, by and large, are not backed up with serried [closed] ranks of jet bombers."

He then defined the strength of this gathering of the leaders of the poor and backward nations as:

"We, the peoples of Asia and Africa, 1,400,000,000 strong, far more than half of the population of the world, we can mobilize what I have called the *Moral Violence of Nations* in favor of peace. . . ."

And where was this moral violence coming from? Sukarno knew to what he was appealing, for he said:

"Religion is of dominating importance particularly in this part of the world. There are perhaps more religions here than in other regions of the globe. . . . Our countries were the birthplace of religions."

And what bound these diverse peoples together? Sukarno said:

"Almost all of us have ties to common experience, the experience of colonialism."

Sukarno was appealing to race and religion; they were the only realities in the lives of the men before him that he could appeal to. And, as I sat listening, I began to sense a deep and organic relation here in Bandung between race and religion, *two of the most powerful and irrational forces in human nature.* Sukarno was not evoking these twin demons; he was not trying to create them; he was trying to organize them. . . . The reality of race and religion was there, swollen, sensitive, turbulent. . . .

It was no accident that most of the delegates were deeply religious men representing governments and vast populations steeped in mystical visions of life. Asian and African populations had been subjugated on the assumption that they were in some way biologically inferior and unfit to govern themselves, and the white Western world that had shackled them had either given them a Christian religion or else had made them agonizingly conscious of their old, traditional religions to which they had had to cling under conditions of imperialist rule. Those of them who had been converted to Christianity had been taught to hope for a freedom and social justice which the white Western world had teasingly withheld. Thus, a racial consciousness, evoked by the attitudes and practices of the West, had slowly blended with a defensive religious feeling; here, in Bandung, the two had combined into one: *a racial and religious system of identification manifesting itself in an emotional nationalism which was now leaping state boundaries and melting and merging, one into the other.* . . .

The results of the deliberations of the delegates at Bandung would be, of course, addressed to the people and the statesmen of the Western powers, for it was the moral notions—or lack of them—of those powers that were in question here; it had been against the dominance of those powers that these delegates and their populations had struggled so long. After two days of torrid public speaking and four days of discussions in closed sessions, the Asian-African Conference issued a communiqué. It was a sober document, brief and to the point; yet it did not hesitate to lash out, in terse legal prose, at racial injustice and colonial exploitation.

I repeat and underline that the document was addressed to the West, to the moral prepossessions of the West. It was my belief that the delegates at Bandung, for the most part, though bitter, looked and hoped toward the West. . . . The West, in my opinion, must be big enough, generous enough, to accept and understand that bitterness. The Bandung communiqué was no appeal, in terms of sentiment or ideology, to Communism. Instead, it carried exalted overtones of the stern dignity of ancient and proud peoples who yearned to rise and play again a role in human affairs.

It was also my conviction that, if this call went unheeded, ignored, and if these men, as they will, should meet again, their appeal would be different. . . . IN SUM, BANDUNG WAS THE LAST CALL OF WESTERNIZED ASIANS TO THE MORAL CONSCIENCE OF THE WEST!

If the West spurns this call, what will happen? I don't know. . . . But remember that Mr. Chou En-lai stands there, waiting, patient, with no record of racial practices behind him. . . . He will listen.

10

JOSEPH KIRIRA AND JOSIAH KARIUKI

Song of Africa (Kenyan Song)

1957

The immediate aftermath of independence saw efforts in many decolonized countries to preserve as much information about the anticolonial struggle as possible. This was particularly true in places such as Kenya, where harsh repression of such activities had rendered primary sources rare (see Map 2, page 5). In much of the colonized world as well, the vast majority of people were illiterate and thus unable to express themselves in writing. Traditionally, historians focus on primary source evidence that was written at the time the events in question took place. In an effort to recover voices that might be lost to history, oral historians seek to use subsequent interviews and testimonials to obtain information about how people understood what they lived through. This is one way scholars work to get access to viewpoints that official sources ignore.

From Josiah Mwangi Kariuki, *Mau Mau Detainee* (Oxford, U.K.: Oxford University Press, 1963), 123–24.

Josiah Mwangi Kariuki published this song in 1963, the year Kenya became independent. His activism against British rule began in the late 1940s, when he became involved in Jomo Kenyatta's Kenya African Union (KAU). After the British declared a state of emergency in 1952, which outlawed the KAU and all political groups in the colony, Kariuki became a local official in the Land and Freedom Army (LFA), which the British called the Mau Mau (see Documents 12 and 13). He was arrested in 1953 and remained in jail until 1960. This song, Kariuki reports, was composed by his fellow LFA detainees in 1957 in response to news of Ghana's independence from British rule. It suggests that these detainees saw their own activities in a larger African context.

God gave to the black people
This land of Africa
Praise the God who dwells in the high places
For his blessings

Chorus:
We will continue in our praises
Of the land of Africa
From East to West
From North to South

After much suffering
The country of Egypt
Was delivered from bondage
And received Freedom

Abyssinia [Ethiopia] saw the light
Shining down from the North
Her people struggled mightily
And rescued themselves from the mire[1]

Now do we loudly rejoice
To hear the story of Ghana
The flag of Great Britain
Has been lowered for all time there

---

[1] Ethiopia had been the last country in Africa to escape European colonial rule, until the Italian Fascists conquered it in 1935. Ethiopian and British troops drove the Italians out in late 1941, but it was not until 1944 that international recognition of Ethiopia's sovereignty was renewed.

If you look round the whole of Kenya
It is only a river of blood
For we have our one single purpose
To lay hold of Kenya's freedom

Listen to the sobbing
Of our brothers in South Africa
Where they are being tormented
By the tribe of Boers [also known as Afrikaners]

We shall greatly rejoice
In the unity of all the black people
Let us create in our unity
A United States of All Africa.

3

From Possibilities of Independence to Expectations of Liberation

11

Song for Murang'a Women (Kenyan Song)
ca. 1950

Many women played key roles in rejecting colonial rule. Often their resistance took what scholars term "everyday" forms, such as feigning ignorance, pretending to follow official rules (but making intentional mistakes), and foot-dragging. Yet some women were also directly involved in other activities that even hostile authorities—who tended to view "everyday" resistance as signs of stupidity, laziness, or incompetence—recognized as political. This song, which circulated in anticolonial circles among the Kikuyu people of Kenya, captures a display of both types of resistance.

Because large numbers of Kikuyu men were itinerant laborers, traveling the country to find work, women bore the brunt of caring for both small family farms and herds. After World War II, in the name of improving the agricultural output of their colony, British authorities in central Kenya ordered all cattle herders to vaccinate their livestock and used forced labor to "terrace" hilly but fertile land by erecting stone walls to slow erosion. The efforts of numerous individual women to avoid participating in these endeavors led to harsh crackdowns by both British officials and, more commonly, the local chiefs whom the British supported. In this context, the Kenya African Union (KAU), which relied on mass mobilization to pressure the British to take account of popular discontent about landownership and growing misery, was able to convince thousands of

---

"Rwa Atumia A Murang'a," in Gakaara wa Wanjaû, ed., *Nyimbo Cia Mau Mau* (Karatina, Kenya: Gakaara Press, 1988), 13–14. Translation by Muoki wa Mbunga.

women around the town of Murang'a to refuse to take part. Their protest begin in the summer of 1947 and continued through 1951. British officials immediately saw this as a significant threat to their authority. It was of particular concern because the women actively ignored their local chiefs, whom the British had counted on as "traditional authorities." The harsh penalties participants suffered and, more broadly, the failure of KAU-led mass action to shape British policy would be key factors in the rise of the Land and Freedom Army (LFA), or Mau Mau (see Documents 12 and 13).

As women of Kikuyu, we were taken to Murang'a
Because we had refused to have our cows and
   goats vaccinated.
And upon refusing, we were all imprisoned.

Chorus:
   Our children cried a lot as they had no milk to suckle.
   Oh God, we beseech you to emancipate us from this slavery.

When we got to prison, they dressed us in white uniforms
And asked us, "Are you the movement that is
   demanding freedom?"

Many patriots who were already in prison gathered at
   the entrance to our cell
Because they were shocked to hear children wailing.

After dressing us, they moved us to Tambarare
   [lowland area].
There we found fellow patriots, who were moved
   away as soon as we arrived.

We fell asleep, and just before dawn porridge was
   brought in a bucket.
There was nothing to drink from, and so we drank it
   from our hands.

And when it was 8 a.m., we saw soldiers in formations.
They ordered us to quickly start clearing the grass
   that was around us.

12

Historical Survey of the Origins and Growth of Mau Mau, 1950

1960

In many colonies, the question of access to land crystallized wider debates about how foreign rule helped some and hurt others. In Kenya, such concerns focused on the area the British called "Happy Valley," where British and European settlers established massive plantations. These settlers received much help from the British government, which had banned Africans from growing coffee, Kenya's most lucrative cash crop. After World War II, the British both encouraged further white immigration and authorized a small number of African landowners to grow coffee. These developments exacerbated the anger of the large majority of local people who had no access to land (see Document 11). Many had been forced either to migrate to cities or to work on the plantations, which had been established on their people's ancestral lands.

It was in this context that Jomo Kenyatta, a radical nationalist, returned from exile to lead the Kenya African Union (KAU). His leadership mobilized large numbers of the discontented, especially among his own Kikuyu people. The KAU targeted not only the British colonial authorities but also the tribal chiefs and elders who received British support and implemented British rules.

The following description of developments in 1950 comes from a 1960 British parliamentary report. As such, it offers evidence from two different moments in Kenya's decolonization, as the author deploys archival sources from ten years earlier to legitimate the report's criticisms of the Land and Freedom Army (LFA), or what the British called the Mau Mau. The LFA was a secret organization that starting in late 1949 slowly coalesced out of a series of distinct groupings. Beginning with the Kikuyus, each of these LFA groups organized through secret "oathing," in which both men and women swore binding oaths to serve the movement and its goals. All of the groups' goals were consonant with those of Kenyatta's KAU, with a focus on landownership and a call for Europeans to leave Kenya. Their relationship to Kenyatta remains unclear, but by 1950

From F. D. Corfield, *Historical Survey of the Origins and Growth of Mau Mau* (London: HMSO, 1960), 100.

the British government was convinced that the LFA was the secret—and violent—arm of Kenyatta's militant organization.

Note how this document begins with a report about LFA secret rites, refers to a second report that asserts a link between the Mau Mau and the Kikuyu Independent School Association (KISA), which was allied with the KAU, and then turns to a third report that shows pro-KAU propaganda in one school. Another telling element here is the description of women's roles in the LFA. Women played a substantial part in most anticolonial movements, but they were particularly prominent in the LFA; some even became guerrilla fighters. Observe how the document presents women's involvement as evidence of the danger British officials saw in the Mau Mau.

1950 closed with reports from most districts of the Central Province and the settled areas of the Rift Valley Province of continued but covert *Mau Mau* activity, but one fresh manifestation appeared before the end of the year. Both the Provincial Police Headquarters and the District Commissioner, Nyeri, reported that:—

> A number of creditable sources of information have reported that the singing of night-time "sympathy" hymns for those who have been imprisoned for illegal *Mau Mau* oath activities has commenced in many parts of the Kikuyu reserve. These hymns, which are said to be sung chiefly by women, also contain words of prayer for the families of convicted members of the *Mau Mau*. At one of these "singing ceremonies," which took place near Mangu in the reserve above Thika on the night following the passing of sentence upon Solomon Memia, a hymn was sung which was worded as follows—

> The first drops of Kikuyu blood have now been shed. The blood of the people of God (*Mumbi*) will stain the grass upon which our cattle grazes before our children can be free.

So far, it is understood, these "singings" have been done in secrecy with every effort being made to avoid both the chiefs and the headmen hearing of them.

The District Commissioner, Kiambu, also stated:—

> There can be little doubt but that the splinter movement in the K.I.S.A. [Kikuyu Independent School Association] schls [*sic*] is closely allied to the *Mau Mau*. It would appear that Jomo's master plan is to mould Kikuyu youth on the totalitarian method in these schools, while these same schools should be used as initiation grounds for the adults at night into extreme forms of Kikuyu nationalism, under

the various titles of *Mau Mau*, Willy Jimmy Kiama, K.C.A. [Kikuyu Central Association], etc.

An interesting sidelight on the above is an earlier report by a District Officer, Community Development, Nyeri, who, while visiting a C.C.M. [Catholic Consulate Mission] school at Kiagunyu on 7th June found a "quiz" in progress on the following lines: —

Q. Who is our leader?   A. Jomo Kenyatta. (Applause.)
Q. Which is the organization   A. K.A.U.
   which helps us?
Q. Are the West Africans our   A. Yes, we are all coloured
   friends?   brothers together.
                                         Etc., etc.

13

Historical Survey of the Origins and Growth of Mau Mau, 1952

1960

Between 1950 and 1953, the Land and Freedom (LFA) movement killed close to two thousand African civilians, two hundred members of the police and British armed forces, and thirty-two white settlers. To stop the movement, the British pursued a massive imprisonment and interrogation campaign, which began in 1950. All adult Kikuyus were presumed to have "oathed" to the Mau Mau (see Document 12), and they had to prove that they had not done so. Anyone who failed to present evidence that she or he had not oathed was required to go through a reeducation process and to swear a counter-oath. This campaign ended in 1959. Estimates of the number of Kenyans who died in the British prison camps are in the tens of thousands; one recent U.S. study suggests that upwards of 100,000 died. Hundreds of thousands of people lost everything they owned, and many were tortured.

The following excerpt from a 1960 parliamentary report presents British arguments as to why overwhelming force and massive violence

From F. D. Corfield, *Historical Survey of the Origins and Growth of Mau Mau* (London: HMSO, 1960), 167.

were necessary in 1952. Most historians contest the premises of these arguments, which suggest that all (or even many) LFA members acted in such a fashion. It is true, however, that shocking forms of violence were embraced by some associated with the LFA, who sought to maximize the impact of their limited capacity for violence. Here, as in the previous document, women's militancy is particularly vilified. Accusations that non-Europeans were sexually perverted and prone to sexual violence—alongside other unspeakable horrors—were typical of colonialist propaganda.

. . . With the onset of active terrorism, two new versions of the oath were devised to meet the needs of the campaign, although there were of course many variations. The first, called the *githaka* or forest oath, was administered by forest gang leaders to their followers. The second, which was introduced towards the end of 1953, the *batuni* or platoon oath, was administered to all *Mau Mau* soldiers and soldier recruits. By taking the *batuni* oath, the man became a full-blooded terrorist. The following are some of the common features of the *batuni* oath:—

a.   to burn European crops, and to kill European-owned cattle.

b.   To steal firearms.

c.   If ordered to kill, to kill, no matter who is to be the victim, even one's father or brother.

d.   When killing, to cut off heads, extract the eyeballs and drink the liquid from them.

e.   Particularly to kill Europeans.

As the terms of the *Mau Mau* oath became increasingly more violent and bloodthirsty, it was not surprising therefore that there was a corresponding increase in bestiality in the ritual of the oath, thus forcing the initiate to reach the necessary pitch of blood lust and degradation to make it possible for him to pronounce the ghastly words of the oath itself. These ceremonies were repeated at intervals to spur the recipients onto greater excesses. It is not possible to give any detailed description of these terrible ceremonies. Suffice to record that the use of menstrual blood and public intercourse with sheep and adolescent girls were a common feature of most of these ceremonies. The necessary number of young women were kept with the gangs for this specific purpose. Concoctions of the foulest and almost unimaginable ingredients were eaten and drunk.[1] The effect of these orgiastic ceremonies, which took place in deep forest clearings by the flickering light of bonfires, on those present must have been overwhelming.

[1] The full physical details of the ceremonies performed to produce these concoctions can hardly be printed in a public document. It is sufficient to record that for one of the more notorious concoctions, known as the "Kaberichia cocktail," semen produced in public was mixed in a bowl with menstrual and sheep's blood and drunk while repeating the oath. Later on in the Emergency, the medical authorities had the greatest difficulty in combating a serious outbreak of typhoid in the big detention camp at Manyani, where oathing continued to take place, as the administrators made use of urine and faeces for their abominable night-time ceremonies. [Note in original—Ed.]

14

GAMAL ABDEL NASSER

Egypt's Liberation: The Philosophy of the Revolution

1955

Gamal Abdel Nasser was the leading figure among a group of young officers who in 1952 overthrew the Egyptian monarchy, a regime headed by King Farouk and supported by British arms and advisers. The name given to this coup d'état was the July 23 Revolution, and over the next several years, as Nasser took control of the new Egyptian republic, he sought to define a revolutionary agenda to explain what was happening. The following excerpts appeared in a collection of autobiographical reflections by Nasser on the "philosophy of the revolution," which was immediately translated into English. It became the focus of much attention when, in 1956, Nasser ordered his troops to nationalize the Suez Canal. This attempt to nationalize the canal led to the Suez Crisis when France and Great Britain supported an Israeli invasion of Egypt to take control of the canal. The crisis was a crucial turning point in the era of decolonization,

From Gamal Abdel Nasser, *Egypt's Liberation: The Philosophy of the Revolution* (Washington, D.C.: Public Affairs Press, 1955), 32–35, 39–43, 83, 84–87.

as the United States rejected calls from its allies to support their actions,
which resulted in the humiliating withdrawal of British, French, and
Israeli forces and Nasser's nationalist triumph.

Before July 23rd, I had imagined that the whole nation was ready and prepared, waiting for nothing but a vanguard to lead the charge against the battlements, whereupon it would fall in behind in serried [closed] ranks, ready for the sacred advance towards the great objective. And I had imagined that our role was to be this commando vanguard. I thought that this role would never take more than a few hours. Then immediately would come the sacred advance behind us of the serried ranks and the thunder of marching feet as the ordered advance proceeded towards the great objective. I heard all of this in my imagination, but by sheer faith it seemed real and not the figment of my imagination.

Then suddenly came reality after July 23rd. The vanguard performed its task and charged the battlements of tyranny. It threw out Farouk and then paused, waiting for the serried ranks to come up in their sacred advance toward the great objective.

Symbol of the Revolution

For a long time it waited. Crowds did eventually come, and they came in endless droves—but how different is the reality from the dream! The masses that came were disunited, divided groups of stragglers. The sacred advance toward the great objective was stalled, and the picture that emerged on that day looked dark and ominous; it boded danger. At this moment I felt, with sorrow and bitterness, that the task of the vanguard, far from being completed, had only begun.

We needed order, but we found nothing behind us but chaos. We needed unity, but we found nothing behind us but dissension. We needed work, but we found behind us only indolence and sloth. . . .

Weapon in the Hand of Hate

We were not yet ready. So we set about seeking the views of leaders of opinion and the experience of those who were experienced. Unfortunately we were not able to obtain very much.

Every man we questioned had nothing to recommend except to kill someone else. Every idea we listened to was nothing but an attack on some other idea. If we had gone along with everything we heard, we would have killed off all the people and torn down every idea, and there would have been nothing left for us to do but sit down among the corpses and ruins, bewailing our evil fortune and cursing our wretched fate. . . .

The Complete Picture

I confess that this whole situation produced in me a psychological crisis; but the events that followed, and my reflections thereon, together with the real meaning I could adduce from them, tended to ease my distress and set me to seek a justification for this situation, which I found when the whole picture of the motherland's plight rose somewhat clearly before my eyes. This clarification, moreover, brought me the answer to the question which had long bothered me, namely: Was it necessary for us, the Army, to do what we did on July 23rd?

The answer is yes, beyond any subterfuge or equivocation. I can say now that we did not ourselves define the role given us to play; it was the history of our country which cast us in that role.

I can now say that we are going through two revolutions, not one revolution. Every people on earth goes through two revolutions: a political revolution by which it wrests the right to govern itself from the hand of tyranny, or from the army stationed upon its soil against its will; and a social revolution, involving the conflict of classes, which settles down when justice is secured for the citizens of the united nation.

Peoples preceding us on the path of human progress have passed through two revolutions, but they have not had to face both simultaneously; their revolutions, in fact, were centuries apart in time. For us, the terrible experience through which our people are going is that we are having both revolutions at the same time.

Between the Millstones

This terrible experience stems from the fact that both revolutions have attendant factors which clash and contradict violently. To be successful, the political revolution must unite all elements of the nation. Build them solidly together and instill in them the spirit of self-sacrifice for the sake of the whole country. But one of the primary features of social revolution is that it shakes values and loosens principles, and sets the citizenry, as individuals and classes, to fighting each other. It gives free rein to corruption, doubt, hatred and egoism.

We are caught between the millstones of the two revolutions we are fated now to be going through. One revolution makes it obligatory that we unite and love one another, fighting side by side to achieve our ends; the other brings dissension upon us against our desires, causing us to hate each other and think only of ourselves. . . .

Only the Army

. . . In this way, as I have already remarked, it was not the Army which defined its role in the events that took place; the opposite is closer to the truth. The events and their ramifications defined the role of the Army in the great struggle to free the nation.

I have been aware since the beginning that our unity is dependent upon our full realization of the nature of circumstances in which we found ourselves, the historical circumstances of our country. For we could not alter the circumstances by the mere stroke of a pen, nor could we turn back the hands of the clock, or advance them—we could not control time. It was not within our power to stand on the road of history like a traffic policeman and hold up the passage of one revolution until the other had passed by in order to prevent a collision. The only thing possible to do was to act as best we could and try to avoid being ground between the millstones. . . .

Geographic Limits

. . . If the whole matter were limited to our capital, or our political boundaries, it would be much simpler. We would shut ourselves in, and live in an ivory tower, and we would try to our utmost to get away from the world, its problems, wars and crises, which all burst in on us through the doors of our country and influence us, though we have nothing to do with them.

The age of isolation is gone.

And gone are the days in which barbed wire served as demarcation lines, separating and isolating countries one from one another. No country can escape looking beyond its boundaries to find the source of the currents which influence it. How it can live with others, how . . . and how. . . .

And no state can escape trying to determine its status within its living space and trying to see what it can do in that space, and what is its field of activities and its positive role in this troubled world. . . .

Fate does not jest and events are not a matter of chance—there is no existence out of nothing. We cannot look at the map of the world without seeing our own place upon it, and that our role is dictated by that place.

Can we fail to see that there is an Arab circle surrounding us—that this circle is a part of us, and we are a part of it, our history being inextricably part of its history.

These are facts and no mere idle talk. Can we possibly ignore the fact that there is an African continent which Fate decreed us to be part of, and that it is also decreed that a terrible struggle exists for its future—a struggle whose results will be either for us or against us, with or without our will? Can we further ignore the existence of an Islamic world, with which we are united by bonds created not only by religious belief, but also reinforced by historic realities? As I have said once, Fate is no jester.

It is not without significance that our country is situated west of Asia, in contiguity with the Arab states with whose existence our own is interwoven. It is not without significance, too, that our country lies in northeast Africa, overlooking the Dark Continent, wherein rages a most tumultuous struggle between white colonizers and black inhabitants for control of its unlimited resources. Nor is it without significance that, when [in the thirteenth century CE] the Mongols swept away the ancient capitals of Islam, Islamic civilization and the Islamic heritage fell back on Egypt and took shelter there. Egypt protected them and saved them, while checking the onslaught of the Mongols at 'Ain Jalut.[1] All these are fundamental realities with deep roots in our lives which we cannot—even if we try—escape or forget.

---

[1] In 1260 CE, near the Sea of Galilee, the Mamluk rulers of Egypt imposed the first durable defeat suffered by Mongol forces in over forty years, which checked the Mongols' southward advance.

15

THE SHIN BET

The Minorities in Israel

February 26, 1958

During the era of decolonization, there was much disagreement about whether colonialism really had ended in certain countries. Often, such criticisms focused on the tight links between the former colonial power and the new government (see Document 14). In several cases, however, critics asserted that the new governments, while clearly independent, were also colonial in nature. This was because they were run by and for people who had emigrated from Europe, so-called settlers. Anticolonialists held up two countries as emblematic of the most racist forms of colonialism under the guise of national independence: South Africa, after its 1948 embrace of apartheid (separation of the races) politics, which worked to exclude all African inhabitants (between 60 and 70 percent of the population) from citizenship; and Rhodesia (now Zimbabwe), which declared its independence from the United Kingdom in 1965 and excluded Africans (about 95 percent of the population) from all political rights (see Map 2, page 5).

The State of Israel, which proclaimed its independence in May 1948 after its victory in a war with surrounding Arab states, also faced accusations that it was a colonial state. Critics argued that various British, European, and U.S. imperialist policies led to its establishment, against the will of the Arab majority of pre-1948 Palestine. Some 50 percent of that group was expelled or fled under duress during the war; afterward, Israel used force and legislation to block the return of those refugees. This helps explain why, in contrast to the white-minority-governed states of South Africa and Rhodesia, a large majority of independent Israel's inhabitants were Jewish (most settlers were of European origin, although growing numbers of Jews came from the Arab world, by choice or because expelled from their homes). Meanwhile, members of Palestine's former majority, Christian and Muslim Arabs, now counted among Israel's minorities. Most enjoyed formal citizenship status and the right to vote,

---

From file 102/GL17013/9, Israel State Archives, Jerusalem. Translation by Shira Robinson with assistance from Yonay Israel.

but unlike Jewish citizens, they lived under a draconian military regime that restricted their access to land, work, and basic civic freedoms.

The following document reveals some of the tensions that resulted from this complicated situation. In early 1958, the Shin Bet, Israel's internal security service, produced this analysis of a struggle within the Israeli Communist party, the country's only legal political organization that included Jews and Palestinians as equal members and was also critical of Zionism, or Jewish nationalism. Known by an acronym of its Hebrew name, MAKI, the party's struggle was typical of debates within Marxist parties across the world in the era of decolonization: how to reconcile claims that all workers shared the same political interests, regardless of origins or national boundaries, with anticolonialist ideology, which increasingly celebrated nationalism and the right to self-determination. The report shows how difficult it was for MAKI to balance its efforts to represent both Jewish and Arab workers while negotiating tensions between Zionism and Arab nationalisms. (There were also tensions between national claims specific to Palestinian Arabs and pan-Arab nationalism; see Document 37.) At the same time, it evokes the Israeli government's difficult balancing act: Using the threat of an Arab national liberation movement domestically in order to marginalize MAKI risked undercutting the authorities' repudiation of the "colonial" or "settler" label that the Arab world imposed on the Jewish state. This was a topic of much discussion in Israel in these years, after Israel's alliance with the United Kingdom and France during the 1956 Suez Crisis and in light of government statements in support of the South African government. It proved particularly intense in early 1958 when, alongside developments detailed here, much of the Hebrew-language press published articles asserting that MAKI's Palestinian leaders were conspiring to undertake "a rebellion on the Algerian model."[1]

During the discussion at the party's Political Bureau, MAKI's Arab leadership brought up for discussion their demand to establish an "Arab movement for national liberation" that would operate independently [from the party]. They proposed two alternatives:

---

[1] Joel Beinin, *Was the Red Flag Flying There? Marxist Politics and the Arab-Israeli Conflict in Egypt and Israel, 1948–1965* (Berkeley: University of California Press, 1990), 199–200; Shira Robinson, *Citizen Strangers: Palestinians and the Birth of Israel's Liberal Settler State* (Palo Alto, Calif.: Stanford University Press, 2013), 176.

a. Establishing the "movement" with MAKI's support and in coordination with the party.

b. In the event of resistance within MAKI, presenting members with a fait accompli, even if this would mean that [Arab leaders] would have to withdraw from the party. They presume, however, that MAKI's progressive national character would eventually force the party to recognize and support the "movement."

The announcement by MAKI's Political Bureau published on 1.27.58 [January 27, 1958] revealed that the party's Jewish majority rejected this demand from the Arab leadership. Yet Arab rank and file, who did not consider the announcement binding, continued to spread the idea of such a "movement" among the Arab population.

The subject was then taken up by the party's Central Committee, which convened between 1.30.58 and 2.1.58. The assembly's decisions, which were published only on 2.7.58, made no mention of the demands of MAKI's Arab leaders. However, based on reports from various sources, as well as on disclosures, interpretations, and articles published by the party's leadership, it is still possible to assert that the rejection of the Arab leadership's demands and the preservation of party unity were achieved — for now — by means of a compromise between the two sides. On one hand, Arab members withdrew their plans to establish a national Arab movement outside the party. On the other, the Jewish side agreed to emphasize [in public statements] the decisions of [MAKI's May 1957] Thirteenth Congress . . . and to demand their implementation: namely . . . (in accordance with the "right to self-determination up to secession") the annulment of the annexation of the territories that Israel [captured beyond the lines of the 1947 UN Partition Plan for Palestine] following the [1948] War of Liberation, on the grounds that the [1949] armistice lines should not be considered the permanent and recognized borders of the State of Israel; and the right of those refugees who used to live in the territory allocated to Israel by the United Nations to return to their homes or receive compensation.[2]

---

[2] The UN Partition Plan for Palestine of November 29, 1947 (Resolution 181), divided the territory of the British mandate of Palestine into three parts: an international zone (Jerusalem and Bethlehem), a Jewish state (around 56 percent of the territory of Mandatory Palestine), and an Arab state (around 43 percent of the territory). After the 1948 war, the armistice agreements between Israel, Egypt, Syria, Lebanon, and Jordan established demarcation lines, which left some 77 percent of the territory of Mandatory Palestine under Israeli control.

These decisions failed to satisfy the radicals in MAKI's Arab leadership, who expressed their position in different ways:

On 2.8.58, committee member Fu'ad Khuri published an article in *al-Ittihad* [the *Union*, MAKI's Arabic-language daily newspaper] concerning the celebrations of Israel's first decade of independence. The topic had been discussed by the Central Committee. After explanations that "ten years ago, all the progressive powers[3] supported the establishment of a democratic and independent state of Israel, as part of the fulfillment of the UN's resolutions from 1947 on the question of *Erets Yisrael*,[4] and in accordance with the right to self-determination of the Jewish people in the Land of Israel/Palestine alongside the right of the Arab Palestinian people to self-determination," it was decided that MAKI would use the occasion of the tenth anniversary to call for the recognition of the national rights of the Arab Palestinian people. But Fu'ad Khuri, whose article was full of incitement against the authorities, was not satisfied to stop there. Instead he went on to claim that the Arab people in Israel had the right to self-determination and the right to unite with the rest of the Arab peoples [a reference to the United Arab Republic, formed one week earlier]. [Khuri] would not count on [governmental] charity to obtain those rights, since "rights are taken, not given." As for [Israel's] tenth anniversary, Khuri asserted that the authorities sought to involve the Arabs of Israel in the celebrations as a way to squeeze out of them a "certificate of good behavior for their executioners" and that any Arab who might participate would be considered a traitor to his people.

In the same issue [of *al-Ittihad*], Deputy Emile Habibi [a Palestinian member of the Knesset, Israel's parliament] published an article in which he called on the Arabs of Israel to prepare for the reunification of the Arab Palestinian people. On the following day, 2.8.58, . . . Habibi spoke at a popular gathering in 'Arrabe [a large Palestinian village in the eastern Galilee], where he proclaimed that the recognized borders of the State of Israel are those designated by the 1947 partition map and that it was only natural that the Arab masses would intensify their struggle for their national rights. "Get ready! The train is approaching the station; can't you hear its whistle blow?"

At the meeting of the [party's] Nazareth District Committee, held on 2.7.58, the following was decided: to stand openly for the unification of

---

[3] For members of MAKI, "progressive powers" referred to the Soviet Union and its Eastern European allies in the United Nations, which all voted in support of the 1947 partition plan.

[4] This Hebrew term translates literally as "the Land of Israel." In this context, it refers to the territory of Mandatory Palestine (1923–1948).

all Arab countries; to discourage the Arab population from participating in the tenth anniversary celebrations; and to establish popular national committees in every Arab village and town, which would represent the Arab people in Israel in the future.

In the meantime, [government] representatives continued to issue warnings to various sections of the Arab public—including those likely to be used as a tool in the hands of MAKI activists, as well as dignitaries, religious leaders, and [non-MAKI] political figures—to underscore [to them] the danger that the establishment of the "Arab movement for national liberation" would pose to the Arabs of Israel.

On 2.6.58, the editors of Israeli newspapers were informed about both the developments within MAKI's Arab sector and the party's internal struggle. The next day . . . when the Central Committee's decisions and the articles by Habibi and Fu'ad [Khuri] were published, the Israeli press launched a comprehensive campaign of warnings and information which covered the emerging plans of MAKI's Arab activists and their activities on the ground; the danger they posed to the Arab minority; and the authorities' determination to eradicate at the root any evidence of activities that threatened state interests.

Following these warnings and the campaign of the entire Israeli press, MAKI's spokesmen began to publicly distance themselves from the separatist plans of MAKI's Arab politicians and to restrict their activity. Indications to this effect were visible in various pieces published in *Kol ha-'Am* [*Voice of the People*, the party's Hebrew-language daily newspaper] from 2.14.58, as well as in the speeches by Jews and Arabs at the celebration of the newspaper's twenty-first anniversary, held on 2.14.58. In an article published in *Kol ha-'Am* on 2.14.58, Emile Habibi argued that "there is no one in the Israeli Communist party who calls for the destruction of Israel" and that all attempts to damage the unity of the party would fail. In the same issue, Meir Vilner [member of the Knesset] denied the existence of [secessionist] plans by Arab activists in MAKI and "explained" the media's attacks on the party as an effect of its effort to defend the government's policy toward the Arab minority. *Kol ha-'Am* also "explained" Fu'ad Khuri's incendiary article in *al-Ittihad* as a denunciation of the military governor's attempt to use the tenth anniversary celebrations to mask [the government's] policies of repression and discrimination against the Arab minority. . . . The Nazareth District Congress, scheduled for 2.14.58 to affirm the resolutions of the District Committee from 7.2.58, was delayed. Despite this, MAKI members in Nazareth were told that the Arab sector would not join the tenth anniversary celebrations, while the Jewish side would exploit the year[-long celebration] to call for the end to discrimination against the Arabs of Israel and to highlight MAKI's positions concerning Israeli-Arab relations and the problems of the Arabs of Israel.

MAKI's leadership made an effort to display the unity of the party, with all the members of the Political Bureau—including the Arab members—participating in the ceremony held in Tel Aviv to mark the anniversary of the founding of *Kol ha-'Am*.

MAKI's Arab cells were instructed not to discuss political matters that contradict the party's platform. In the Jewish sector, all reports concerning a plan to establish a separatist movement were denied. The entire matter was explained in terms of a Shin Bet provocation.

In conclusion, it is possible to say that for now the plan to establish an "Arab movement for national liberation" has been abandoned. In return for the withdrawal by MAKI's Arab activists of their demand [for recognition of their right to national self-determination and unity with other Arabs]—and in order to maintain the unity of the party—MAKI will emphasize the right to self-determination of the Arabs of Israel (in accordance with the resolution of the Thirteenth Congress, which has not been publicized until now), . . . and the temporary nature of the current [post-1948] borders of the State of Israel.

16

GEORGIOS GRIVAS

Report Addressed to Michail Christodolou Mouskos

May 23, 1955

Among anticolonial activists, post-1945 developments raised enormous expectations that the end of imperial rule was imminent, not just in India or Indonesia, but in their countries as well. By the early 1950s, however, it seemed clear to many that the United Nations, which had proved both unwilling to intervene in most colonial situations and ineffective in doing so, and the two superpowers, which had moved away from earlier

From "Extracts from the Captured Grivas Diaries," *Journal of Cyprus Studies* (January 2007).

anticolonial efforts, had left them on their own and still under foreign rule. For some, a growing sense of deception and impatience led to a new radicalism. This was particularly visible in Cyprus, an island in the eastern Mediterranean whose inhabitants were split between Turkish-speaking Muslims and Greek-speaking Orthodox Christians, but which had been under British control since 1878.

In April 1955, a previously unknown group, the National Organization of Cypriot Combatants (known by the initials of its Greek name, EOKA), which sought the end of British rule and union with Greece (called enosis*), began a bombing campaign to achieve its ends. The following excerpt is from a cache of documents that British forces discovered and arranged to publish. They were written by one of the organization's key leaders, Georgios Grivas, a Cypriot-born general in the Greek army who was known in the EOKA by his nom de guerre, Digenis. In late 1954, he noted in his private journal: "The first news from the UNO [UN] is unfavorable for Greece. America's position is against us and after this we should expect nothing from [the] UNO. What is going to happen now? Our wise diplomats who were boasting that a solution would be found through the UNO, what do they intend to do now?" Several months later, the EOKA began to pursue a campaign of violent attacks, which used bombs and firearms to target civilians who supported British rule or simply provided services to the government. This report was addressed to "Gen," the code name for Michail Christodolou Mouskos, also known as Archbishop Makarios III, leader of the Cypriot Orthodox Church. An ardent supporter of* enosis, *Makarios became the first president of the independent Republic of Cyprus in 1960.*

I wish to acquaint you with the situation as it is presented today, as well as with the repercussion of the events, which started on April 1st, on the decisions and actions of the Government of Cyprus and the Turks of Cyprus.

I thought it necessary to bring this to your knowledge so that you, as the real Leader of the National Liberation Struggle, may make decisions, after having known the events and not under the influence of men of politics or of the party. I do this because it has come to my knowledge, or rather I have been informed from Greece by a person with whom I have no connection at all, that there have been various behind-the-scenes activities in Athens in connection with the ongoing militant struggle, and that some demand my removal from here. . . .

The experience of the national struggle, which I have been conduct-ing for 15 years, has made me capable of seeing clearly the things con-nected with it and of looking at their results rationally, not only on the field of war but also in terms of the repercussions which they have on the political and diplomatic fields.

I shall not try to speak to you about the past and about the mistakes made simply because of the intervention of certain persons, but I shall confine myself to speaking to you about the present, how the situation is developing today and what my plans are for the future. You will then be the person most competent to decide.

The Government Measures

In addition to the repressive military and police measures the Govern-ment has taken, which are unlikely to be effective in case of a general uprising, they have also taken preventive measures, the object of which is to paralyze our activity in advance so that it cannot happen, or can happen only halfheartedly. These measures are at least as threatening as the repressive ones, if not more serious, and we must think seriously how to face and neutralize them. These measures are the following:

a. Assassinations of leaders of the movement and especially of Your-self. A letter which was sent to the Turkish leaders in Cyprus, and which I tend to believe the Government sent, contains the following:

"Instead of shouting, you had better murder the Archbishop because then the Greeks will be occupied with the election of a new Archbishop and refrain from the *Enosis* movement. . . ."

What Should Be the Future Plan of Action?

Our plan must include a total and co-ordinated use of all means at our disposal, i.e., sabotage in the towns and the countryside. Cutting off of communications as well as attacks on rural police stations and, if pos-sible, on army camps. Simultaneous uprisings and disturbances on the part of pupils and peasants. The struggle must be organized in such a way so that it may last at least until next October, when the Cyprus ques-tion will be discussed in the UNO [UN].

This plan will be executed in stages. On the one hand we shall dis-perse, fatigue and irritate the enemy and on the other hand we shall see how we can reach the final stage of the plan without running the risk of seeing our struggle suppressed prematurely and before October.

So: At the beginning we shall organize acts of sabotage in the towns and in important communication centres, with simultaneous attacks on police stations, especially on mountainous areas, in order to compel the enemy to disperse its forces.

If this effort is crowned with success, then we shall go on with activity by small groups of armed men in mountainous areas which will make sudden attacks and then hide themselves. The targets will be police stations and Army camps.

Finally, if the above are crowned with success, we shall organize a general rising of the youth in the towns and the country [through] militant demonstrations. The organized population will also participate. These militant demonstrations are being organized by us.

These are my views on general lines on the present situation in Cyprus and on our potentialities.

Of course, the above general plan, and the means which will be used for its successful execution, require more detailed study and, after they are connected with diplomatic demands, we could make the necessary modifications. The thing, however, which does not accept any modification is the need for continuation of the militant struggle which has started, because its abandonment will mean that the *Enosis* question is buried.

17

Oath of the National Organization of Cypriot Combatants

1955

Like most armed anticolonial movements, the EOKA (see Document 16) depended on loyalty and secrecy. The oath that its male and female members took sought to legitimate both the organization's aims and means. Note how it insists on national unity as well as obedience to the EOKA's authority.

From "Extracts from the Captured Grivas Diaries," *Journal of Cyprus Studies* (January 2007).

—Comandar, why have they [the French authorities] arrested those men?

—Because, dear child, in their eyes, we are guilty.

—But not always. . . . They should punish those who are guilty and not those who are not.

—But son, we are all guilty; that is who we are. So they punish some with bullets, the others with beatings or prison; their words make some suffer, others are starved. They kill with every move they make. They chase our people from the light, away from the land that they cultivate; and we do not even take notice. When they fling one of our dead down before us, only then do we understand. We take pity on this man whom they have killed; faced with him we are ashamed. But we, too, we are being pushed toward the tomb; . . . we are ready to climb in, with no word uttered, not the slightest movement to escape.

—That's horrifying!

—No it's not. Today it's horrifying. Tomorrow it will be different. Look at the big farmers who of are our kind, the city merchants who are also of our kind. They say nothing. When a man falls in this struggle . . . each one of them shuts up for a moment. They get all nervous and breathe a sigh. Once again, of course, each will go his separate way. The cycle begins again. For each has but one route open. It's a bit narrow, I'll admit.

—What needs to happen to make things different? Do you know?

—We must eliminate abuses, bury them. . . . Without them, there would not be any more reasons to be ashamed when faced with the living than when faced with . . . our dead.

—That's all?

—That is enough for a start.

—But there are so many more of us, Omar said.

—Of course there are more of us. Among that number there are the thin and the fat, the little and the big, the timid and the daring. . . . There are so many of us! But the courageous men among us who are prepared to take the first step, they need much patience.

Comandar's words, burning and gentle, entered the boy's heart like a long nail.

—But if no one declares his readiness to die, Omar said, then everyone will suffer.

—I said nothing, the old man replied. We must be linked one to the other as if by a chain.

—What I think is that they're a mean bunch when you get down to it. . . .

—This is why the malicious must be eliminated.
—So, is that all?
—That's all, little man.

19

NATIONAL LIBERATION FRONT

Proclamation

November 1, 1954

The small group of men who launched a series of violent attacks across Algeria's territory on November 1, 1954, sought to alter existing relationships: the relationship between France and Algeria and also the relationships among Algerians. Their decision to use violence to target agents and symbols of colonialism signaled their rejection of previous strategies, which had remained within the legal channels that the French state had established and that had been pursued by other nationalists. The following statement was distributed secretly in Algiers on November 1, 1954. It was accompanied by a second tract from the National Liberation Army (ALN), the armed wing of the National Liberation Front (FLN), which had carried out the attacks. At this point, the same men ran the two groups, but note the importance they attached to distinguishing between the political and military organizations. The proclamation lays out their goals while affirming as self-evident the basis of those goals. Its fundamental purpose was to establish the political grounds for armed struggle against those who impeded Algerian independence: French authorities, on the one hand, but certain Algerians, on the other, notably those who claimed to be struggling for Algerian independence as well.

The "two clans" the proclamation targets were opposing groups within the Movement for the Triumph of Democratic Liberties (MTLD, the initials of its French name), a nationalist anticolonial party founded in 1946. One group, the Messalistes, supported the "father of Algerian nationalism," Messali Hadj, the charismatic founder of the MTLD, who

From Henri Alleg, ed., *La guerre d'Algérie* (Paris: Editions Temps Actuels, 1981), 3: 507–11. Translation by author.

was under house arrest in France. The second group, the Centralistes, supported members of the party's Central Committee, who challenged Messali's domination of the party. The men who founded the FLN were closer to the Centralistes, but the key experience they shared was membership in the MTLD's Special Organization, a paramilitary group that had been banned and crushed by French authorities in 1949. With their actions and proclamations of November 1, 1954, the FLN (and its twin, the ALN) affirmed that it alone incarnated the national struggle: Others could join it — in fact, they were ordered to do so — but only under FLN leadership. While the Centralistes, for the most part, quickly did so, the Messalistes, notably Messali Hadj, completely rejected this claim. His supporters would form the Algerian National Movement (MNA), which continued to contest the FLN's authority and engaged in often violent conflicts with the FLN — until the war's end.

To the Algerian people

To the Militants of the National Cause

To you who are called upon to judge us, the Algerian people in general, the militants in particular, our purpose in distributing this proclamation is to enlighten you concerning the underlying reasons that impelled us to act by revealing to you our program, the meaning of our action, and the cogency of our views, all of which remain focused on the goal of National Independence within the North African framework. We also wish to help you avoid succumbing to the confusion that imperialism, through its corrupt political and administrative agents, will surely seek to spread.

It is our understanding, first, that after decades of struggle the National Movement has reached its final stage, that of realization. In effect, as the goal of the revolutionary movement was to create all of the conditions necessary to launch the liberation fight, it is our estimation that: internally, the people have united around the call for independence and struggle; externally, the climate of détente [between pro-American and pro-Soviet blocs] offers a favorable context to settle minor problems (among them ours), particularly since we can count on the diplomatic support of our Arab and Muslim brothers. The events in Morocco and Tunisia are significant in this regard[1] and have profoundly altered how the liberation struggle is unfolding in North Africa. It is worth noting

[1] See the headnote to Document 20.

that we have been, and for quite some time, at the fore of efforts to unite our struggles. Unfortunately, such unity among the three countries has yet to be realized.

Today, [Moroccans and Tunisians] have headed fearlessly down this path, and relegated to the rear, we suffer the fate of those whom events have left behind. This is how our National Movement—overwhelmed by years of stasis and the force of habit, poorly directed, cut off from the indispensable support of public opinion, and overtaken by events—has progressively disintegrated, to the great satisfaction of colonialism, which thinks it has won its most important victory in its struggle against the Algerian vanguard. The hour is dire.

Confronted with this potentially irreparable situation, a group of young leaders and astute activists, who were able to rally around them most of the healthy and decisive elements of the National Movement, has decided that the moment has come to escape from the impasse into which personal struggles and fights over influence trapped us, in order to launch, alongside our Moroccan and Tunisian brothers, a veritable revolutionary struggle.

To this end, we want to make clear that we are independent of the two clans that are fighting over power [within the National Movement]. Placing national interest above all petty and erroneous considerations of personality and prestige, in conformity with revolutionary principles, our action is directed solely against colonialism, our only enemy, blind and obstinate, which has always avoided any extension of even the most minor liberties [when confronted] through peaceful means.

These are, we think, sufficient reasons for our movement of renewal to present itself under the name of NATIONAL LIBERATION FRONT. In this way, we distance ourselves from any possible compromise and offer the possibility to all Algerian patriots, from all social milieus, to all parties and movements that are wholly Algerian, to integrate them-selves into the struggle for liberation, without any other consideration.

To make clear who we are, we spell out below the key axes of our political program:

GOAL: NATIONAL INDEPENDENCE BY:

The restoration of the sovereign, democratic, and social Algerian
   state, within the framework of Islamic principles.
The respect of all fundamental liberties without distinction of race
   or religion.

INTERNAL OBJECTIVES:

A cleansing of politics, by putting the National Revolutionary Movement back on its true path and by wiping out every last remnant of corruption and reformism, the causes of our current backwardness.

The gathering together and organization of all the healthy energies of the Algerian people in order to liquidate the colonial system.

EXTERNAL OBJECTIVES:

The internationalization of the Algerian problem.

The realization of North African unity within its natural Arab-Islamic framework.

Under the framework proposed by the UN Charter, the affirmation of our active sympathy with regard to all nations that would support our liberation struggle.

MEANS OF STRUGGLE:

In conformity with revolutionary principles, and taking into account the internal and external situations, the continuation of the fight by any means until our goal is realized.

In order to reach these objectives, the National Liberation Front will have two essential tasks to carry out actively and simultaneously: an internal struggle, on the fronts of politics and of actual fighting; and an external struggle, with the support of all our natural allies, aimed at making the Algerian problem a real issue for the world.

This is a heavy task that necessitates the mobilization of all national energy and resources. It is true that the fight will be long, but the end result is certain.

Finally, in order to avoid all false interpretations and subterfuges, in order to prove our real desire for peace, to limit the number of human lives lost and the amount of blood spilled, we propose to French authorities an honorable basis for negotiations, if the latter act in good faith and recognize once and for all that the peoples they have conquered have the right of self-determination:

The opening of negotiations with the authorized spokesmen of the Algerian people on the basis of a recognition of Algerian sovereignty, whole and indivisible.

A climate of confidence must be created through the liberation of all political prisoners, the lifting of all exceptional measures, and the end of all efforts to track [our] fighting forces.

The recognition of Algerian nationality by an official declaration repealing the edicts, decrees, and laws that present Algeria as a "French land," which is a denial of the history, the geography, the language, the religion, and the customs of the Algerian people.

IN RETURN:

Those French cultural and economic interests that were honestly acquired will be respected, as will persons and families.

All French people wishing to remain in Algeria will be able to choose between their nationality of origin, in which case the law will treat them as foreigners, and Algerian nationality, in which case they will be considered as such in their rights and obligations.

The links between France and Algeria will be defined and will be the object of an agreement between the two powers on the basis of equality and mutual respect.

Algerian! We invite you to reflect on the charter we define above. It is your duty to make it your own in order to save our country and restore it to freedom. The National Liberation Front is your front. Its victory is yours.

As for us, resolved to pursue the struggle, confident of your anti-imperialist sentiments, we give the best of ourselves to the Fatherland.

THE SECRETARIAT
Proclamation of the F.L.N.
1 November 1954

20

FRANÇOIS MITTERRAND

Speech in Response to FLN Actions

November 12, 1954

*The French government that confronted the National Liberation Front's
armed revolt of November 1, 1954 (see Document 19), had come to
power just months earlier, under the leadership of the center-left politician
Pierre Mendès-France. What brought him to power was the North
Vietnamese armed forces' humiliating defeat of the French army at Dien
Bien Phu on May 7, 1954. Almost immediately, the new government
opened peace negotiations with Viet Minh (North Vietnamese) and other
Indochinese (South Vietnamese, Laotian, Cambodian) leaders. By July,
they had signed the Treaty of Geneva, which led to the formal division of
Vietnam into North and South and French withdrawal from Indochina.
Concurrently, Mendès-France began a process that by autumn 1954
extended "internal autonomy" to the French protectorates of Tunisia and
Morocco. France also officially recognized that its five small colonies
on the coast of India would join the Republic of India. This, then, was
the larger context of the following remarks about Algeria made in the
National Assembly on November 12 by François Mitterrand, the French
minister of the interior (in charge of policing and public order within
France) and future president of France.*

Ladies and gentlemen, I am sure that after this debate the National
Assembly would like to know as precisely as possible how the events
under discussion took place. What happened is that during the night
of October 31 to November 1st, all across Algerian territory, from Constantine to Algiers and from Algiers to Oran, there were armed attacks,
bombings, the sabotage of lines and routes of communication, the light-
ing of fires as well.

In the Department of Constantine, as you know, the most serious
incidents occurred. There, five people were killed—one officer, two

From *Les grands débats parlementaires de 1875 à nos jours, rassemblés et commentés par
Michel Mopin—Notes et études documentaires* (Paris: La Documentation française, 1988),
311–12. Translation by author.

on-duty soldiers, a *caïd* [Muslim judge], and a teacher—under conditions as have been evoked by earlier speakers and that, it cannot be emphasized enough, had a deeply symbolic character. [Two] young teachers had come to pursue—and it was their first day—the vocation they had embraced. And suddenly they are struck down. Would they have known why? Undoubtedly not, things happened quickly. Assassinated, they did at least have time to witness a Muslim, a brother, as he tried to defend them and who was the first to die.

I choose to believe that, as we speak, some are worriedly meditating on this hastily launched outburst, which has forced them into a difficult situation, one that will end badly for them. And [yet] now all around us, out of nowhere, the idea is spreading that Algeria is in chaos.

Is it Algeria's turn, just like Morocco and Tunisia, which experienced this phenomenon of individual terrorism in their cities and in the countryside? Must Algeria, too, enter into the cycle of this world that for the last fifteen years is in revolt against the nations that claimed to be their guardians?

Well, in fact, no, that is not what will happen! Because it so happens that Algeria is France; because it so happens that Algeria's departments are departments of the French republic. From Flanders [on the Belgian border] to the Congo, if there is some difference in how our laws are applied, the law still reigns everywhere, and that law is French law; it's the law that you [deputies] vote, because there is only one parliament and one nation in our overseas territories, just like the departments of Algeria, just like in the metropole.

That is the rule that guides us, not just because the constitution requires it, but because this is how we want it to be.

No one here has the right to claim that the government of the republic hesitated in its duties, not even for one instant, because the actions we took reflect the very essence of our politics.

The prime minister [Pierre Mendès-France] said it this afternoon: How is it possible to explain the deal to end French involvement that we were forced to conclude in Asia, other than through devious conspiracies, if you do not accept that we acted there in conformity with the principles that, collectively, we defined, wrote down, and proclaimed? Our goal was to hold on to the French domain, this domain that stretches, in a meaningful way, as I just stated, from Flanders to the Congo.

That's what we hold to be true; it's the guiding principle of our policies. This is why there is nothing contradictory in negotiating treaties, because that is what was necessary, in Geneva and in fighting when that, too, is necessary, in the Aurès Mountains [of Algeria] or anywhere that there is an attempt to eliminate, to destroy, [or] to attack our homeland's unity.

We immediately took action. You will allow me, I imagine, not to give details. But I see no risk in telling the National Assembly, as I told the Commission for the Interior, that in less than three days we have transported to Algeria sixteen Republican Security Companies [armed mobile police units; in 1954, each company had roughly two hundred men], which brings the number stationed on Algerian territory to twenty.

In three days, this deployment had been completed. Some asked: Is it to keep the peace? It's more than that. It is an affirmation of French power and a sign of our voluntarism. The main goal is not repressive; it is not a military-style counterattack aimed at reconquering territory, which we haven't even lost! It is directed at local populations who could be worried, as a guarantee that at any instant, at every moment, they will be defended.

21

SLIMANE AZEM

Locust, Leave My Country (Berber Song)

1955

By the mid-1950s, Algerian musicians had gained new popularity in France. Most sang in Kabyle Berber, the language spoken by most of the hundreds of thousands of poor workers who had left the misery of Algeria's rural areas to work in metropolitan factories, mines, and construction jobs. Alongside the traditional themes of love and beauty, Kabyle songs also evoked exile—the forced departure of workers from their home villages in order to provide for their families—and, after 1945, nationalist politics. Slimane Azem, who began recording in 1949, lived in Paris with his French wife. Many of his songs were explicitly political. The one that follows was widely played on Radio-Paris, a public radio station, during the hours dedicated to Arabic and Kabyle music. When it was first heard

"Criquets, quittez mon pays!" From Mehenna Mahfoufi, ed., *Chants kabyles de la guerre d'indépendance. Algérie 1954–1962 (Kabyle Songs of the War for Independence: Algeria, 1954–1962)* (Paris: Seguier, 2002), 180–81. Translation by author.

in early 1956, listeners responded enthusiastically: Its allegorical call for the French to leave Algeria had made it through the censors. A number of other versions, recorded by different artists during the war for Algeria's independence, made the song's implications much more explicit. Azem's version, however, remained the best known, although a controversy over whether he supported the National Liberation Front or a competing nationalist group, the Algerian National Movement (see Document 19), ruined his reputation in Algeria after independence. Azem died in France in 1983.

I had a walled garden, where everything grew marvelously
There were peaches, there were pomegranates
I worked there when the sun beat down, even basil did I grow
It so flourished that you could see it far away
The crickets they rushed in, to devour everything
Eating right down to the roots.

Locust, leave my country, its former wealth is now all gone
If the courts sold it to you really, then produce an authentic bill of sale

Locust, you have drained my country, and I ask myself how come?
You have ripped out the heart and wasted the hard work of our fathers
Even if you turned into a dove, peace between us would not come

You came down from the sky, like beating snowflakes
You ate the grain and the stems, and devoured the tastiest treats
Leaving just the chaff, as if I was an ass.

Locust, know your limits, take the measure of your worth,
Prepare yourself to leave and go back from where you came
If not, do take care, because you'll pay for your misdeeds

Locust, you sicken me, a heartache you give to me
With your larvae you infest the grain that should be mine
But the hour of the locust is now ending, my destiny is back in my
    hands.

22

MUSLIM POPULATION OF TÉBESSA

Letter to Robert Lacoste
July 1956

In 1956, the Algerian city of Tébessa, which abuts the Tunisian frontier to the east (see Map 2, page 5), had a population of around twenty thousand; the overwhelming majority were Muslims. The role of Islam was important during the Algerian conflict, notably in the rhetorical battle over Algerian independence. French critics of Algerian nationalism claimed that it was not a real nationalism, but merely a combination of Muslim fanaticism and anti-European racism. Nationalists argued that France would never give Algerians full rights because they were Muslims and that French claims to pursue "universal" values camouflaged disdain and disregard for Arabs and Muslims. This letter suggests the power of such understandings. It was addressed to the top French civilian official in Algeria, Resident Minister Robert Lacoste.

Those responsible for the protection of the Muslim religion were served [on July 20, 1956] with an expulsion decree from the local administration, which gave them eight hours to clear the premises.

This expulsion decree made no distinction between buildings reserved for community use and those that lodge religious personnel.

The authorities then proceeded with a series of searches, during which blasphemous acts were committed, with no regard for the spiritual values of our faith.

Everything was destroyed, up to and including the holy word of the Qu'ran.

What these facts clearly demonstrate is that this was not a security measure, but its opposite, an expression of deep hatred toward all that is Muslim, for all that is Arab, which is to say all that is Algerian. What was done reveals a violent, provocative disdain for our holy religion.

From Algerian National Archives Fonds GPRA-MAE 54.1.15. Translation by author.

Can we still turn for justice to existing authorities, to protest against this anarchical tyranny that relies on religious criteria in pursuit of racial discrimination?

We want to believe we can, and so we submit our solemn and indignant protest.

23

RENÉ MASSIGLI

French Intelligence Analysis of British Public Opinion on the Algerian Conflict

December 1956

French officials were very concerned that their allies might drop their support for French efforts to hold on to Algeria or, even worse, begin to support the National Liberation Front (FLN). They used every means at their disposal to keep this from happening. France insisted that all efforts to develop European integration—including the 1956 Treaty of Rome, which established the European Economic Community, as well as the earlier North Atlantic Treaty Organization (NATO), founded in 1949—treat Algeria as an extension of France and thus of Europe. They worked hard, and for several years successfully, to prevent the United Nations from taking up the Algerian question, with the claim that it was a purely domestic affair.

Alongside diplomatic efforts, the French government pursued an international public relations campaign, which included sending speakers and films about Algeria—dubbed in English or Spanish—around the world, with Western Europe and the Americas, North and South, particular targets. French officials also complained bitterly to U.S. officials that American college campuses and church groups were welcoming FLN spokesmen who justified "terrorist violence." As part of their public relations campaign, the French used various approaches to influence local audiences, notably by framing their arguments in reference to specific national histories and expectations. In 1960, for example, a French

From French National Archives 552AP (Auriol Papers), 156. Translation by author.

minister explained on the American television news show Meet the Press *that in Algeria, France was following "the Hawaiian way" by making this overseas land a full-fledged part of the French republic.*

The following document, which was prepared for other French officials by René Massigli, the secretary-general of the Ministry of Foreign Affairs, analyzes the attitudes of the "average Englishman" about Algeria; it also suggests how French officials could frame their arguments to influence this man's opinion. Note how it proposes to distinguish Algeria from other territories that had decolonized while also comparing it to certain British colonies where the United Kingdom resisted independence movements. In his effort to defend French policy, Massigli includes a quotation from a 1930s article by the Algerian leader Ferhat Abbas, a moderate nationalist who had recently joined the FLN and who later became the first president of the Provisional Government of the Algerian Republic (GPRA), proclaimed in Tunis in 1958. After the article was published, Abbas said that he had been misinterpreted, and he subsequently rejected the statement as inaccurate.

The average Englishman has only vague ideas about the Algerian problem.

Until last year, he had no doubt that Algeria was an integral part of France, with three departments that followed the same administrative model as the metropole and elected legislators, some of European and some of native origins, to the National Assembly [the lower house of the French parliament] and the Council of the Republic [the upper house].

The ongoing agitation, its amplitude and its resemblance to a civil war, have shaken him. Going to the other extreme, he now sometimes tends to think of Algeria as an Arab nation, just like Tunisia and Morocco, and legitimately able therefore to expect the same recognition of its independence.

Among the many points that might be brought up to enlighten him, the average Englishman would undoubtedly be open to arguments that highlight the many similarities that exist between the Algerian question and certain problems that Great Britain is facing in the Commonwealth.

a. As in South Africa, the extremely rapid expansion of the native population, along with the slow growth of the European population, poses problems. Over the last fifteen years this has led to a serious and growing disequilibrium between the two sections of the Algerian population.

France, we might underline, is not looking to solve this via a policy similar to apartheid, which is wholly contrary to our traditions. [France] is working to bring different points of view together in the most liberal fashion possible, all while recruiting as many indigenous people as possible to work in the local administration.

b. Algeria's troubles are quite similar, in their origins and in how they are playing out, to those the Mau Mau caused in Kenya. The same undefinable coming together of diverse agitators who launch bloody raids on villages, farms, even urban centers, where they commit horrific crimes, marked by the most savage cruelty, then disappear into the mountains. England did not falter and after long months of steadfast struggle found a way to reestablish order. We hope that we will be able to do the same.

c. For France, Algeria plays an important role, which is not without analogies to the role that Cyprus has for Great Britain.

The stakes, however, are much more significant, as Algeria is only five hundred miles from France and is astride the axis that runs to [French] territories in central and western African. French Africa, from Algiers to Brazzaville, forms a whole, and any fissure in that whole risks undoing it all. Also much like Cyprus, Algerian agitation is primarily inspired and encouraged by outsiders.

By making reference to religious and linguistic communities, they rely on pan-Islamism and pan-Arabism, which have no actual basis in history. They also act as if nothing has happened in 125 years, with their rejection of the immense economic, social, and cultural development that France has undeniably brought to Algeria [since the conquest of Algiers in 1830].

In Cyprus, terrorism would end immediately if the outside agitators could be kept out, if supplies and arms were not constantly smuggled in, and if foreign radios were not constantly summoning forth violence and disorder.

Similarly, in Algeria the vast majority of indigenous people hope only to live in peace and perfect harmony with the Europeans. The summons to hatred and revolt come from abroad; the funds, the arms and munitions, are provided by foreign countries, whose radio programs are full of endless incitation to rebel.

Finally, we might remind people that Ferhat Abbas, who now presents himself as a champion of Algerian nationalism, solemnly declared several years ago in a speech: "I have explored history, and I did not find an Algerian nation."

24

CHARLES DE GAULLE

Presidential Press Conference

April 11, 1961

*The Algerian War brought General Charles de Gaulle back to power in
France, through a rush of events in May and June 1958, which began
with an uprising in support of keeping French Algeria that took over the
city of Algiers, saw the mobilization of French troops, and then witnessed
the collapse of the Fourth French Republic. De Gaulle was named prime
minister and proposed a new constitution, which hewed closely to the
project he had been calling for since 1945 and gave the president of the
republic unprecedented powers. De Gaulle became president in early
1959. His personal authority was already substantial: In 1940, he had
established a French government-in-exile (the Free French) to fight on
against the Germans after their conquest of France, and he had maneuvered, against U.S. disapproval, to include France on the side of World
War II's winners rather than its losers. With his prestige joined to the
power of the presidency, much of the world quickly came to believe that
France was, once again, a force to be reckoned with.*

*Although ardent supporters of keeping Algeria part of France had
created the conditions of his return, de Gaulle had only one goal: French
grandeur, or "greatness." Despite his long-standing support for empire,
he was willing to trade it for other measures of international power and
prestige. The following excerpt from a press conference he gave clearly
indicates that by April 1961, he was ready to accept Algeria's independence. Not everyone agreed: Just days later, a failed coup d'état by French
military officers (the second since de Gaulle returned to power) sought
to oust the president in order to defend French Algeria. The war itself
continued on for another year.*

*Like other leaders who succeeded in these years, from Harold Mac-
millan of Great Britain (see Document 30) and Gamal Abdel Nasser
of Egypt (see Document 14) to Kwame Nkrumah of Ghana (see Docu-*

From *Major Addresses, Statements and Press Conferences of General Charles de Gaulle:
May 19, 1958–January 31, 1964* (New York: French Embassy, Press and Information
Division, 1964), 113–17.

ment 39) and Eric Williams of Trinidad and Tobago (see Document 27),
de Gaulle narrated the past in ways that gave listeners a sense that his
decisions were coherent and resulted from active choices rather than
from circumstances beyond his control. This heroic style of leadership was
particularly popular in these years, in the formerly colonized countries as
well as in the so-called developed world.

I should like it to be well understood that in France's policy toward Algeria, the following essential idea must be faced squarely: in the world of
today and in the times in which we live, France has no interest whatsoever in maintaining under her jurisdiction and under her dependence
an Algeria which would choose another destiny, and it would not be
in France's interest to be responsible for the population of an Algeria
which would have become master of its own fate and would have nothing to offer in exchange for what it would ask. The fact is that, to say the
least, Algeria costs us much more than it is worth to us. Whether in the
matter of administrative expenses, economic investments, social welfare, cultural development or the many obligations with regard to the
maintenance of law and order—what we furnished to it in effort, money
and human ability has no counterpart that anywhere nearly approaches
it.

It must in the same way be realized that France's present responsibilities in Algeria constitute heavy military and diplomatic burdens for
her. And that is why France would consider today with the greatest calm
a solution whereby Algeria would cease to be a part of France—a solution which in former times might have seemed disastrous for us but
which, I say it again, we consider with a perfectly calm mind. . . .

. . . There are people who will say: "But it is the rebellion which leads
you to think in this way." . . . It is not this that makes me speak as I do; I
do not deny that the events which have occurred, which are occurring
in Algeria have confirmed what I have thought and demonstrated for
more than twenty years, without any joy of course—and you can well
understand why—but with the certainty of serving France well.

Since Brazzaville,[1] I have not ceased to affirm that the populations
dependent on us should have the right to self-determination. In 1941, I

[1] In 1944, as World War II drew to a close, the Free French government sponsored
the Brazzaville Conference (in present-day Congo). De Gaulle and some forty colonial
administrators attended, with no Africans among them. The conference declaration
proposed a series of reforms for French colonies, including the abolition of forced labor,

granted independence to the mandated States of Syria and Lebanon. In 1945, I gave all Africans, including Algerian Muslims, the right to vote. In 1947, I approved the Statute of Algeria which, if it had been applied, would probably have led to the progressive institution of an Algerian State Associated with France. . . . I agreed that the protectorate treaties concerning Tunisia and Morocco should be approved. . . . In 1958, having resumed leadership, I, along with my Government, created the Community[2] and later recognized and aided the independence of the young States in Black Africa and Madagascar. Not having returned to power in time to prevent the Algerian insurrection, immediately upon my return I proposed to its leaders to conclude the peace of the brave and to open political talks. . . .

[During 1958, 1959, and 1960,] . . . I and my government have not ceased to act in order to promote a Muslim leadership in Algeria and to put the Muslims in a position to take local affairs into their own hands, until such time as they are able to take over on the government level. . . .

In conclusion what does this add up to: to decolonization. But if I have undertaken and pursued this task for a long time, it is not only because we could foresee and later because we witnessed the vast movement toward freedom which the world war and its aftermath unleashed in every corner of the globe, and which the rival bids of the Soviet Union and America did not fail to emphasize. I have done it also, and especially, because it seemed to me contrary to France's present interests and new ambition to remain bound by obligations and burdens which are no longer in keeping with the requirements of her strength and influence.

Moreover, this is true for others as well. It must be recognized that in the great transformation which is taking place from one end of the universe to the other, the itching for independence of erstwhile dominated peoples and also the incitements thrown out by all the demagogues of the world are not the only motivating forces. There is another which is not always very clearly perceived because of habits of mind, but which is nonetheless a very positive factor, one that is growing and tending to become the predominant one, especially in France. I mean that the reasons which once led certain civilized peoples to take under their direct control certain other peoples which were not—these reasons are disappearing even from the minds of the ex-colonizers. . . .

---

increased educational opportunities for colonial subjects, and greater control of local affairs by the people in each colony. Independence, however, was not included.

[2] The French renamed their empire after World War II, first calling it the French Union (1946–1958), then the French Community.

France does not have to be at all sorry for what she has achieved overseas in this capacity and in this form. I have said it often and I repeat: it constitutes a great human accomplishment which—notwithstanding certain abuses and errors and despite all the endless spouting of all sorts of worthless demagogues—will forever be a credit to France. But how many things have changed today.

Now our great national ambition is our own national progress, constituting a real source of power and influence. Now the modern era permits us, compels us, to undertake a vast development. Now for this development to succeed we must first of all employ the means and resources at our disposal on our own behalf, in our own country. All the more so as we need these means and resources to ensure our own defense and that of our neighbors against the greatest imperialism that the world has ever known—the imperialism of the Soviet Union. We also need these means to win out in the tremendous economic, technical and social struggle now under way between the forces of humanity and the forces of slavery.[3]

It is a fact: our interest, and consequently our policy, lies in decolonization. Why should we continue to cling to costly, bloody and fruitless domination when our country has to undergo complete renovation, when all the underdeveloped countries, beginning with those which yesterday were our dependencies and which today are our favorite friends, ask for our aid and our assistance? But this aid and this assistance—why should we extend them if it is not worthwhile, if there is no cooperation, if what we give finds no return? Yes, it is a matter of exchange, because of what is due us, but also because of the dignity of those with whom we are dealing.

[3] This is his description of the cold war.

25

FRANTZ FANON

The Wretched of the Earth

1961

A man of mixed European and African heritage, the influential writer, psychiatrist, and activist Frantz Fanon was born a French citizen on the Caribbean island of Martinique (still legally part of France). He trained as a psychiatrist in Lyon and in 1953 became director of a psychiatric hospital in Algeria, where he found himself when the National Liberation Front (FLN) began its anticolonial struggle. Fanon's confrontation with French racism led him to write extensively on what it meant for him and others to be forced to think of themselves as black rather than as simply human, which he argued deformed all people. As a philosopher, he remains important for his efforts to identify the foundations of what he termed "Manichaean thinking": how terms such as white *and* black, *or* native *and* colonizer, *came to confine people in polarized relationships. His aim was to open the possibilities of more complex, and more fully human, understanding for all people.*

During the three years he directed the hospital in Algeria, Fanon came to see that Algeria's independence struggle offered revolutionary possibilities. In 1957, he moved to Tunis, where the FLN was then headquartered. He continued to practice psychiatry but also wrote for the organization's official newspaper and participated in FLN discussions. He later served as ambassador to Ghana for the Provisional Government of the Algerian Republic (GPRA) (see Document 26). Drawing on his understanding of what revolutionary action could mean, Fanon published his final book, excerpted here, in 1961.

Fanon's goal in The Wretched of the Earth *was to provide an ideological road map that would allow colonized people to benefit from the cascading series of decolonizations. His prescriptions sought to avoid the dangers inherent in any struggle that took place on the national level and to allow the global revolt against colonial racism's "thingification" of the colonized to succeed. In his preface to Fanon's book, the French*

From Frantz Fanon, *The Wretched of the Earth*, trans. Richard Philcox (New York: Grove Press, 2004), 1–8, 52, 57–59.

philosopher Jean-Paul Sartre proclaimed that "the Third World finds itself *and speaks to* itself *through his voice." Because it offered a convincing alternative to Marxism's privileging of the proletariat and of class relations, the book immediately became a touchstone for New Left radicals in Western Europe and the United States. Fanon did not live to witness the response to* The Wretched of the Earth; *within months of its publication, he died of leukemia.*

On Violence

National liberation, national reawakening, restoration of the nation to the people or Commonwealth, whatever the name used, whatever the latest expression, decolonization is always a violent event. At whatever level we study it—individual encounters, a change of name for a sports club, the guest list at a cocktail party, members of a police force or the board of directors of a state or private bank—decolonization is quite simply the substitution of one "species" of mankind by another. The substitution is unconditional, absolute, total, and seamless. We could go on to portray the rise of a new nation, the establishment of a new state, its diplomatic relations and its economic and political orientation. But instead we have decided to describe the kind of tabula rasa [blank slate] which from the outset defines any decolonization. What is singularly important is that it starts from the very first day with the basic claims of the colonized. In actual fact, proof of success lies in a social fabric that has been changed inside out. This change is extraordinarily important because it is desired, clamored for, and demanded. The need for this change exists in a raw, repressed, and reckless state in the lives and consciousness of colonized men and women. But the eventuality of such a change is also experienced as a terrifying future in the consciousness of another species of men and women: the *colons*, the colonists.

. . . Decolonization is the encounter between two congenitally antagonistic forces that in fact owe their singularity to the kind of reification secreted and nurtured by the colonial situation. Their first confrontation was colored by violence and their cohabitation—or rather the exploitation of the colonized by the colonizer—continued at the point of the bayonet and under cannon fire. The colonist and the colonized are old acquaintances. And consequently, the colonist is right when he says he "knows" them. It is the colonist who *fabricated* and *continues to fabricate* the colonized subject. The colonist derives his validity, i.e., his wealth, from the colonial system.

Decolonization never goes unnoticed, for it focuses on and fundamentally alters being, and transforms the spectator crushed to a nonessential state into a privileged actor, captured in a virtually grandiose fashion by the spotlight of History. . . . The "thing" colonized becomes a man through the very process of liberation.

Decolonization, therefore, implies the urgent need to thoroughly challenge the colonial situation. Its definition can, if we want to describe it accurately, be summed up in the well-known words: "The last shall be first." Decolonization is verification of this. At a descriptive level, therefore, any decolonization is a success. . . .

The colonized world is a world divided in two. The dividing line, the border, is represented by the barracks and the police stations. In the colonies, the official, legitimate agent, the spokesperson for the colonizer and the regime of oppression, is the police officer or the soldier. In capitalist societies, education, whether secular or religious, the teaching of moral reflexes handed down from father to son, the exemplary integrity of workers decorated after fifty years of loyal and faithful service, the fostering of love for harmony and wisdom, those aesthetic forms of respect for the status quo, instill in the exploited a mood of submission and inhibition which considerably eases the task of the agents of law and order. . . . In colonial regions, however, the proximity and frequent, direct intervention by the police and the military ensure the colonized are kept under close scrutiny, and contained by rifle butts and napalm. We have seen how the government's agent uses a language of pure violence. The agent does not alleviate oppression or mask domination. He displays and demonstrates them with the clear conscience of the law enforcer and brings violence into the homes and minds of the colonized subject. . . .

. . . The colonist's sector is a sector built to last, all stone and steel. It's a sector of lights and paved roads, where the trash cans constantly overflow with strange and wonderful garbage, undreamed-of leftovers. The colonist's feet can never be glimpsed, except perhaps in the sea, but then you can never get close enough. They are protected by solid shoes in a sector where the streets are clean and smooth, without a pothole, without a stone. The colonist's sector is a sated, sluggish sector, its belly is permanently full of good things. The colonist's sector is a white folks' sector, a sector of foreigners.

The colonized's sector, or at least the "native" quarters, the shanty town, the Medina, the reservation, is a disreputable place inhabited by disreputable people. You are born anywhere, anyhow. You die anywhere, from anything. It's a world with no space, people are piled one on top of the other, the shacks squeezed tightly together. The colonized's sector is a famished sector, hungry for bread, meat, shoes, coal, and light. The colonized's sector is a sector that crouches and cowers, a sector on its knees, a sector that is prostrate. It's a sector of niggers, a sector of towel heads. The gaze that the colonized subject casts at the colonist's sector is a look of lust, a look of envy. Dreams of possession. Every type of possession: of sitting at the colonist's table and sleeping in his bed, preferably with his wife. The colonized man is an envious man. The colonist is aware of this as he catches the furtive glance, and constantly on his guard realizes bitterly that: "They want to take our place." And it's true there is not one colonized subject who at least once a day does not dream of taking the place of the colonist.

This compartmentalized world, this world divided in two, is inhabited by different species. The singularity of the colonial context lies in the fact that economic reality, inequality, and enormous disparities in lifestyles never manage to mask the human reality. Looking at the immediacies of the colonial context, it is clear that what divides this world is first and foremost what species, what race one belongs to. In the colonies the economic infrastructure is also a superstructure. The cause is effect: You are rich because you are white, you are white because you are rich. This is why a Marxist analysis should always be slightly stretched when it comes to addressing the colonial issue. It is not just the concept of the precapitalist society, so effectively studied by Marx, which needs to be reexamined here. The serf is essentially different from the knight, but a reference to divine right is needed to justify this difference in status. In the colonies the foreigner imposed himself using his cannons and machines. Despite the success of his pacification, in spite of his appropriation, the colonist always remains a foreigner. It is not the factories, the estates, or the bank account which primarily characterize "the ruling class." The ruling species is first and foremost the outsider from elsewhere, different from the indigenous population, "the others."

The violence which governed the ordering of the colonial world, which tirelessly punctuated the destruction of the indigenous social fabric, and demolished unchecked the systems of reference of the country's economy, lifestyles, and modes of dress, this same violence will be vindicated and appropriated when, taking history into their own hands, the colonized swarm into the forbidden cities. To blow the colonial world to smithereens is henceforth a clear image within the grasp and imagination of every colonized subject. To dislocate the colonial world does not mean that once the borders have been eliminated there will be a right of way between the two sectors. To destroy the colonial world means nothing less than demolishing the colonist's sector, burying it deep within the earth or banishing it from the territory.

Challenging the colonial world is not a rational confrontation of viewpoints. It is not a discourse on the universal, but the impassioned claim by the colonized that their world is fundamentally different. The colonial world is a Manichaean world. The colonist is not content with physically limiting the space of the colonized, i.e., with the help of his agents of law and order. As if to illustrate the totalitarian nature of colonial exploitation, the colonist turns the colonized into a kind of quintessence of evil. Colonized society is not merely portrayed as a society without values. The colonist is not content with stating that the colonized world has lost its values or worse never possessed any. The "native" is declared impervious to ethics, representing not only the absence of values but also the negation of values. He is, dare we say it, the enemy of values. In other words, absolute evil. A corrosive element, destroying everything within his reach, a corrupting element, distorting everything which involves aesthetics or morals, an agent of malevolent powers, an unconscious and incurable instrument of blind forces. . . .

Sometimes this Manichaeanism reaches its logical conclusion and dehumanizes the colonized subject. In plain talk, he is reduced to the state of an animal. And consequently, when the colonist speaks of the colonized he uses zoological terms. Allusion is made to the slithery movements of the yellow race, odors from the "native" quarters, to the hordes, the stink, the swarming, the seething, and the gesticulations. In his endeavors at description and finding the right word, the colonist refers constantly to the bestiary. The European seldom has a problem with figures of speech. But the colonized, who immediately grasp the intention of the colonist and the exact case being made against them, know instantly what he is thinking. This explosive population growth, those hysterical masses, those blank faces, those shapeless, obese bodies, this headless, tailless cohort, these children who seem not to belong to anyone, this indolence sprawling under the sun, this vegetating existence, all this is part of the colonial vocabulary. General de Gaulle speaks of "yellow multitudes," and [Nobel Prize–winning author] Monsieur [François] Mauriac of the black, brown, and yellow hordes that will soon invade our shores. The colonized know all that and roar with laughter every time they hear themselves called an animal by the other. For they know they are not animals. And at the very moment when they discover their humanity, they begin to sharpen their weapons to secure its victory.

As soon as the colonized begin to strain at the leash and to pose a threat to the colonist, they are assigned a series of good souls who in the "Symposiums on Culture" spell out the specificity and richness of Western values. But every time the issue of Western values crops up, the colonized grow tense and their muscles seize up. During the period of decolonization the colonized are called upon to be reasonable. They are offered rock-solid values, they are told in great detail that decolonization should not mean regression, and that they must rely on values which have proved to be reliable and worthwhile. Now it so happens that when the colonized hear a speech on Western culture they draw their machetes or at least check to see they are close to hand. The supremacy of white values is stated with such violence, the victorious confrontation of these values with the lifestyle and beliefs of the colonized is so impregnated with aggressiveness, that as a counter measure the colonized rightly make a mockery of them whenever they are mentioned. In the colonial context the colonist only quits undermining the colonized once the latter have proclaimed loud and clear that white values reign supreme. In the period of decolonization the colonized masses thumb their noses at these very values, shower them with insults and vomit them up. . . .

On Violence in the International Arena

. . . Not so long ago, Nazism transformed the whole of Europe into a genuine colony. The governments of various European nations demanded reparations and the restitution in money and kind for their stolen treasures. As a result, cultural artifacts, paintings, sculptures, and stained-glass windows were returned to their owners. In the aftermath of the war the Europeans were adamant about one thing: "Germany will pay." At the opening of the [Adolph] Eichmann trial [on charges of crimes against humanity, related to his role in the Holocaust] Mr. Adenauer, on behalf of the German people, once again asked forgiveness from the Jewish people. Mr. Adenauer renewed his country's commitment to continue paying enormous sums to the state of Israel to compensate for Nazi crimes.[1]

---

[1] [Fanon] And it is true that Germany has not paid in full the reparations for its war crimes. The compensation imposed on the conquered nation has not been claimed in full because the injured parties included Germany in their anti-Communist defense system. . . .

At the same time we are of the opinion that the imperialist states would be making a serious mistake and committing an unspeakable injustice if they were content to withdraw from our soil the military cohorts and the administrative and financial services whose job it was to prospect for, extract and ship our wealth to the metropolis. Moral reparation for national independence does not fool us and it doesn't feed us. The wealth of the imperialist nations is also our wealth. At a universal level, such a statement in no way means we feel implicated in the technical feats or artistic creations of the West. In concrete terms Europe has been bloated out of all proportions by the gold and raw materials from such colonial countries as Latin America, China, and Africa. Today Europe's tower of opulence faces these continents, for centuries the point of departure of their shipments of diamonds, oil, silk and cotton, timber, and exotic produce to this very same Europe. Europe is literally the creation of the Third World. The riches which are choking it are those plundered from the underdeveloped peoples. The ports of Holland, the docks in Bordeaux and Liverpool owe their importance to the trade and deportation of millions of slaves. And when we hear the head of a European nation declare with hand on heart that he must come to the aid of the unfortunate peoples of the underdeveloped world, we do not tremble with gratitude. On the contrary, we say among ourselves, "it is a just reparation we are getting." So we will not accept aid for the underdeveloped countries as "charity." Such aid must be considered the final stage of a dual consciousness—the consciousness of the colonized that *it is their due* and the consciousness of the capitalist powers that effectively *they must pay up.*

26

VISITOR

Lift Up the Torch of United Africa

April 12, 1958

*In the late 1950s, anticolonialists increasingly focused on the question of
what tactics were acceptable in the pursuit of their goals. India's independence (1947) continued to inspire many, especially the embrace by the
Indian National Congress of nonviolence (usually linked to the leadership
of Mohandas Gandhi). Yet the armed struggle that the National Liberation Front (FLN) had begun in Algeria, which provoked widespread
condemnation in the West, and the harsh violence that colonial powers
deployed to defend their control sparked an intense debate in anticolonial
circles around the world.*

*Ghana seemed to prove that the Indian model could work in Africa.
In 1957, the former British colony became the first European colony on
the continent to win independence (see Map 2, page 5). This came after
many years of intense pressure on the British by labor unions and political activists, who together had formed the Convention People's Party
(CPP). As in India, their approach was nonviolent; similarly, the process
that led to independence was well-ordered and had resulted from negotiations. The leader of the CPP, Kwame Nkrumah, became the new country's
first prime minister (see Document 39).*

*Nkrumah presented developments in Ghana to the world as an African
rethinking of the Gandhian model, which he called "positive action." In
the speech he gave on Independence Day (March 6, 1957), he reminded
Ghanaians, "Our independence is meaningless unless it is linked up
with the total liberation of Africa." In mid-April 1958, he convened the
first Conference of Independent African States to organize toward this
end. Along with leaders of Egypt, Ethiopia, Ghana, Liberia, Morocco,
Sudan, Tunisia, and the United Arab Republic (Egypt), representatives
from various liberation movements attended. The FLN sent a delegation,
which made waves when it directly challenged Nkrumah's arguments in
favor of nonviolent methods.*

From *Evening News* (Accra, Ghana), April 12, 1958.

The following article appeared days before the conference opened. Its anonymous author, "Visitor," strongly supports Nkrumah's critique of colonialism and calls for a "united Africa." Yet the author describes a world in which Nkrumah's positive action approach was no longer sufficient. This distinction was particularly noticeable to Ghanaian readers, as the article appeared in the official newspaper of the CPP, the Evening News, *which usually hewed closely to Nkrumah's views.*

From Algeria in the North to Nigeria in the West, from Kenya in the East to the tribes in the South, Africans bemoan their fate against the atrocities of colonialism! The whole of Africa trembles under the impact of colonial brutalities.

Brutalities from the hands of imperialists who were supposed to have brought Christianity to Africa! It evokes scepticism in the minds of Africans as to whether Christianity was not just a farce. But for our own inner realization of the existence of God, we would have long ago condemned Christianity as an imperialistic [religion]. Fortunately, we are true Christians because of our own inward conviction.

But it is hard to believe that the poor tribes in the South are living in "hell" created on earth by imperialistic Christians who are regular churchians [church attendees]!

The inhuman atrocities directed against the Algerians whose only "crime" is their bid for freedom points the barometer of wilful sin at the French Christians. Just like giving a dog a nasty name in order to make it easy to shoot, the poor Algerians are labelled "terrorists."

If nationalism and terrorism are synonymous then the French, the British, the Americans and the Russians to mention a few, had once been hardened terrorists. After all do the two world wars make sense if not fought for the sole purpose of maintaining the independence and freedom of nations? I would fight and die for my independence rather than live "peacefully" in subservient servitude!

When it is an African uprising against tyranny and oppression the imperialists call it terrorism; but when it is a white people taking up arms under similar conditions they call it a just cause—the recent Hungarian uprising was endorsed universally as a just opposition against suppression and those who engaged in it were christened "freedom fighters."[1]

---

[1] In 1956, the Soviets and their allies sent troops to crush a popular uprising in Hungary that challenged Communist rule.

What the Russians did to the Hungarians that the Free world made so much hue and cry about was the same thing the British did in Kenya [in their fight to crush the Land and Freedom Army] and the French are doing in Algeria. But our shrewd friends the British and French imperialists called theirs a fight against terrorism. As if snatching a man's God-given land from him by force and usurping his rights—the very thing the imperialists are doing—is not worse than terrorism or any other crime!

If last year's [sic] bombardment of Egypt [in the 1956 Suez Crisis] and the recent bombing of poor Sakiet in Tunisia[2] which was a flagrant infringement of the sovereignty of these independent nations were not acts of terrorism then the imperialists' conception of terrorism is faulty!

It is high time we were blunt and impartial in our condemnation of colonialism in Africa, be it from the British, French or any foreign power.

My attack is not against white men or individuals, far from it. The African is Christian enough to treat racialism with the abhorrence it deserves. But my attack is against the imperialistic Governments which advocate colonialism. . . .

When will another Christ come to expose these Pharisees? They call their countries member nations of the "Free-world" yet hitherto they have found it safe not to raise accusing figures [sic] against their friends who are engaged in campaigns of brutal manoeuvres against the sacred freedom of Africans. I hold no brief for Russia and am not interested in the dirty power bloc business [the cold war between the pro-Soviet Eastern bloc and the pro-U.S. Western bloc]. But they are ready to accuse Russia of her brutalities but to them their imperialistic friends are faithful Christians trying to "save" Africa from terrorism. Yes these are the members of the Free-world and of course, they are all honourable nations!

From the foregoing it can be seen clearly that the imperialists' philosophy of existence is white supremacy over Black. Their objective is to make a slave-plantation of Africa.

But Africa, mother Africa, take heart! Haven't you heard the trumpets heralding the good news? Well then listen! Ghana, tiny but mighty Ghana, has pierced the oval-shaped Iron Wall of colonialism![3] The most

[2] On February 8, 1958, the French air force bombed the Tunisian town of Sakiet Sidi Youssef as part of France's efforts to fight the armed rebellion in Algeria led by the FLN. The FLN's army, the National Liberation Army (ALN), had bases in Tunisia, including in Sakiet Sidi Youssef.

[3] The "Iron Wall" is a reference to the iron curtain, the metaphorical name that, in 1945, Winston Churchill gave to the frontier dividing Soviet-dominated Eastern Europe from the "free world," as well as a description with biblical resonance.

hated walls are tumbling down. From east to west, from south to north, Ghana's triumph echoes felicitations of hope to all thy sons and daughters. Look at Kenya! Look at Nigeria! Dr. Aggrey[4] seemed to have risen from his grave and taunting the imperialist saying "I told you so! Catch us if you can!" Africa, dear Africa, take heart.

The imperialists are cornered. The trepid coyotes are shaken to the liver. Names like Nkrumah, Nasser, [Habib] Bourguiba [first president of the Republic of Tunisia], [William V. S.] Tubman [then president of the Republic of Liberia], and [B. Nnamdi] Azikiwe [a leading Nigerian nationalist, who became president at independence in 1960], to mention only a few of Africa's strong men, are scare-crows in the hearts of every imperialist. The forthcoming conference of African Independent States is tipping the scale. They are scared stiff of African unity in which they foresee their remaining colonial wall totally and finally expunged. Yea, they are worried! Yea, they are fluid and will soon be driven to desperation! But in their nauseating temerity they are bound to bring the very thing they fear right on top of them.

Take heart, Africa, we will win. That righteousness always triumphs over callous injustice can never be gainsaid. Arise, Africa, and get ready!

God is on our side. God is always on the side of the righteous. Unlike the imperialists, we are true Christians. We don't covet the lands of other nations. And because we are pure Christians for us it is a gigantic "V" for VICTORY. Long live Africa, Long live her strong men on the scene!!!

Long live the delegates to the African Conference!

---

[4] Dr. J. E. Kwegyir Aggrey (1875–1927) was born in the British colony of Gold Coast (now Ghana) and educated in the United States to be a Methodist missionary. One of Africa's most renowned educators, Aggrey counted Nkrumah among his students.

27

ERIC WILLIAMS

Massa Day Done

March 22, 1961

Between 1945 and 1965, the British-ruled Caribbean, which included thousands of islands as well as the colonies of British Guiana (now Guyana) and British Honduras (now Belize), went through dramatic changes. Mass action by workers in the 1930s, which aimed to reform the conditions of agricultural and industrial workers, had led to the rise of both strong labor unions and nationalist political parties. Over the course of the 1940s, the United Kingdom responded by extending universal adult suffrage across all of its Caribbean colonies. In 1947, the colonial power sponsored a conference in Montego Bay, Jamaica, to explore the establishment of a West Indian federation. The British goal was to define a new relationship between the Caribbean and the United Kingdom, which would meet contemporary challenges to colonial rule by redefining ties rather than ending them.

Many political activists in the Caribbean, including those who were harshly critical of British colonialism, invested their hopes and efforts in plans for a West Indian federation. For some, a reformed relationship with Britain—far away and far less powerful than it had once been—would buffer the region from too much interference from its very close and very powerful neighbor to the north, the United States. The federation, however, never became a reality. Plans collapsed because of tensions among the leaders of the different island territories and the growing certainty that in the Caribbean, as in the rest of the world, national independence was the order of the day. The success of the Cuban Revolution, which in 1959 installed an anti-imperialist government led by Fidel Castro, encouraged such thinking.

Eric Williams played a key role in late 1950s debates about the federation. In 1955, he became the leader of the People's National Movement (PNM) in the two-island territory of Trinidad and Tobago (by far the richest of the islands, due to its oil). He was already well-known as the

---

From *Forged from the Love of Liberty: Selected Speeches of Dr. Eric Williams*, comp. Paul K. Sutton (Port of Spain, Trinidad: Longman Caribbean, 1981), 210–15.

author of Capitalism and Slavery, *a 1948 book derived from his Oxford University dissertation, which revolutionized historical work on the Caribbean. In 1962, he became the first leader of Trinidad and Tobago when it (along with Jamaica) gained independence.*

The following selection is an excerpt from a 1961 speech Williams gave to explain a phrase he had used a few months before, "Massa Day Done." It was one of a series of talks he presented in Woodford Square, a public square in Port of Spain, the capital of Trinidad and Tobago. One particularly important part of this speech was the link he made between the situation of people of African descent, whose ancestors had come to the Caribbean as slaves, and those of South Asian ("Indian") descent, who had come to the region via a system of indentured servitude.

What was Massa Day, the Massa Day that is done? Who is Massa? Massa was more often than not an absentee European planter exploiting West Indian resources, both human and economic. [There is] a book well known to students of West Indian history written by an absentee English landlord who visited his plantations in Jamaica for the first time around 1815. The author's name was Matthew Lewis.[1] He has [*sic*] written a journal of his visits to Jamaica, and in my [previous] address I referred to one passage in the journal when, as he went around the plantation, the slaves ran up to him with all sorts of complaints, saying "Massa this, Massa that, Massa the other." Massa lived in England off the profits of West Indian labor. He became a big shot and ostentatiously flaunted his wealth before the eyes of the people of England.... Massa's children were educated in England at the best schools and at the best universities, and it was openly and frequently claimed in the long period of the British controversy over the abolition of the slave trade and abolition of slavery that Oxford and Cambridge [Universities] were filled with the sons of West Indian Massas. When things got bad and sugar ceased to be king in the West Indies, Massa simply pulled out of the West Indies, in much the same way as the descendants of Massa's slaves today pull out from the West Indies and migrate to the United Kingdom.

We have a record of one such Massa in the small poverty stricken island of Nevis. He arrived in Nevis about 1680 with ten pounds, a quart of wine and a Bible. He developed into a big shot, became planter,

---

[1] Matthew Lewis, *Journal of a West-India Proprietor: Kept during a Residence in the Island of Jamaica* (London: John Murray, 1834).

merchant and legislator, and when things turned sour in the nineteenth century, he invested all his wealth derived from the West Indian soil and the West Indian people in railways and canals and harbors in Canada, India and Australia. He went back to live in the old County of Dorset in England from which his ancestors had migrated to the West Indies, and his biographer tells us that today the same family occupies the same pew in the same church in the same village. What he does not tell us is that it was as if Massa had never emigrated to the West Indies. Massa left behind Nevis as underdeveloped as he had found it. The wealth that should have been ploughed back into Nevis to save it from its present disgrace of being a grant-aided colony, went to fertilize industrial development everywhere in the world except in the West Indies. Today only a beach which bears his name survives to remind us that this particular Massa had ever existed in Nevis. His English biographer tells us that it was as if he had never left his English county. We tell him it is as if Massa had never been in the West Indian island.

On his West Indian sugar plantation Massa employed unfree labor. He began with the labor of slaves from Africa, and [after the 1833 abolition of slavery] followed this with the labor of contract workers from Portugal and China and then from India. The period of Massa's ascendancy, the period of Massa's domination over workers who had no rights under the law, the period of Massa's enforcement of a barbarous code of industrial relations long after it was repudiated by the conscience of the civilized world, lasted in our society for almost 300 years.

To his slave workers from Africa the symbol of Massa's power was the whip, liberally applied; records exist showing that 200 lashes were not infrequent and a tremendous howl was raised by Massa when British law tried to step in and limit punishment to 39 lashes under supervision. To his contract workers from India the symbol of Massa's power was the jail. Massa's slogan was: the Indian worker is to be found either in the field or in the hospital or in jail. For trivial offenses as leaving the plantation without permission, being drunk at work, using obscene language, encouraging his colleagues to strike, the Indian worker, who was paid a legal wage of 25 cents per day, was sentenced to jail by the law of Trinidad and the law of British Guiana where Indians were employed in large numbers. . . .

. . . Massa's long economic domination of the West Indies reduced the population of the West Indies, whether slave, contract or free, to the drudgery of the simplest and most unedifying operations, almost unfitting them totally for any intelligent agricultural activity, and giving them a profound and almost permanent distaste for agricultural endeavors.

Massa was able to do all of this because he had a monopoly of political power in the West Indies which he used shamelessly for his private ends. . . . He used this political power ruthlessly to import workers for his sugar plantations with no respect either for elementary economies of his time or of population problems of the future. Massa's economy was distinguished by perhaps the most scandalous waste of labor the history of the world has ever known. . . .

As far as Massa was concerned this organization of West Indian economy, this dispensation of political power was one of the eternal verities. He developed the necessary philosophical rationalization of this barbarous system. It was that the workers, both African and Indian, were inferior beings, unfit for self government, unequal to their superior masters, permanently destined to a status of perpetual subordination, unable ever to achieve equality with Massa. It was there in all the laws which governed the West Indies for generations—the laws which denied equality on grounds of color, the laws which forbade non-Europeans to enter certain occupations and professions, whether it was the occupation of jeweler or the profession of lawyer, the laws which forbade intermarriage, the laws which equated political power and the robe with ownership of land, the laws which, consciously or unconsciously, directly or indirectly, attempted to ensure that the non-European would never be anything but a worker in the social scale, the improvement of whose standard of living depended, as a British Secretary of State once told the workers in Jamaica in 1865, on their working on Massa's plantation for wages. . . .

Massa was determined to use his political power for his own personal ends. He had no sense of loyalty to the community which he dominated or even to the community from which he had originally sprung. When Massa in Haiti found that the French Government was ready to abolish slavery he offered the island to England. When Massa in Jamaica found that the British were ready to abolish slavery he entered into conspiracy with planters in the southern States of America. . . . Massa was always opposed to independence. He welcomed political dependence so long as it guaranteed the economic dependence of his workers. He was for self government so long as it was self government for Massa only and left him free to govern his workers as he pleased. Our whole struggle for self government and independence, therefore, is a struggle for emancipation from Massa.

That was the West Indian Massa. There has been slavery and unfree labor in other societies. Ancient Greek society, precisely because of slavery, had been able to achieve intellectual heights that so far have had no parallel in human history. The ownership of a large slave empire in the West Indies did not prevent the flowering of intellect and the evolution of politics in the metropolitan countries of Europe. But the West Indian Massa constituted the most backward ruling class history has ever known. Massa in Jamaica had a contempt for education and the profession of teaching which scandalized even the commentators of the eighteenth century. . . . Massa in Trinidad in the early twentieth century asked sarcastically of what use would education be to the children of the plantation workers if they had it. . . .

This was Massa Day. This was Massa—the owner of a West Indian sugar plantation, frequently an absentee, deliberately stunting all the economic potential of the society, dominating his defenseless workers by the threat of punishment or imprisonment, using his political power for the most selfish private ends, an uncultured man with an illiberal outlook.

Massa Day Done everywhere. How can anyone in his senses expect Massa Day to survive in Trinidad and Tobago? For Massa Day Done in Trinidad and Tobago, too, since the advent of the PNM [People's National Movement] in 1956. Let us assess the position in Trinidad today.

Massa's racial complex stunted the economic development of our territories. . . .

Massa stood for the degradation of West Indian labour. PNM stands for the dignity of West Indian labour. The symbol of Massa's authority was the whip, his incentive to labour was the lash. Today, with the PNM, the worker's right to establish trade unions of his own choice and to bargain collectively with his employers is recognized by all but the obscurantist [opponent of intellectual advancement and political reform] who still regards Trinidad, as Massa did, as a place to which the ordinary conventions of human society ought not to apply. Massa passed laws to forbid non-Europeans from being jewellers or lawyers. Today, under the PNM, the right of the West Indian to occupy the highest positions in public and private employment is axiomatic and is being increasingly enforced.

Massa stood for colonialism: any sort of colonialism, so long as it was colonialism. Massa's sole concern was the presence of metropolitan troops and metropolitan battleships to assist him in putting down West Indian disorders. Today, with the PNM, those who were considered by Massa permanently unfit for self government, permanently reduced to a status of inferiority, are on the verge of full control of their internal affairs and on the threshold, in their federation, of national independence.

Massa believed in the inequality of races. Today, as never before, the PNM has held out to the population of Trinidad and Tobago and the West Indies and the world the vision and the practice of interracial solidarity which, whatever its limitations, whatever the efforts still needed to make it an ordinary convention of our society, stands out in sharp contrast as an open challenge to Massa's barbarous ideas and practices of racial domination. Massa was determined not to educate his society. Massa was quite right; to educate is to emancipate. That is why the PNM, the army of liberation of Trinidad and the West Indies, has put education in the forefront of its program. . . .

. . . There are still Massas. Massa still lives with his backward ideas of the aristocracy of the skin. And Massa still has his stooges, who prefer to crawl on their bellies to Massa, absentee or resident, Massa this, Massa that, Massa the other, instead of holding their heads high and erect as befits a society which under the PNM is dedicated to the equality of opportunity and a career open to talent.

5

The Contagion of Independence

28

CONSCIENCE AFRICAINE

Manifesto for Belgian Congo

July 1956

In response to a 1955 proposal by the liberal Belgian writer Antoine van Bilsen for a thirty-year plan for the political liberation of Belgian Africa, a group of Congolese Catholic intellectuals centered in the colonial capital of Léopoldville (now Kinshasa) and associated with the newspaper Conscience Africaine *put forward their own plan for the Belgian Congo (see Map 2, page 5). The Congo's colonial history was particularly violent; it provided the inspiration for Joseph Conrad's bloodcurdling novel* Heart of Darkness *(1899). In addition, Belgian rule had offered almost no chance for the Congolese to benefit from educational or professional opportunities. This Manifesto was not only the first serious response to Bilsen's project; it was also the first clearly political statement by a group of Congolese writers about their country's future. It had, testimonials agree, the effect of a bomb. Copies were posted in villages across the colony, and Congolese from all walks of life excitedly discussed its contents. The claims it stakes out vis-à-vis Belgium seem very moderate today, yet what readers noticed at the time was the daring affirmation that the Congolese people could make choices about their future.*

From Alan P. Merriam, *Congo: Background to Conflict* (Chicago: Northwestern University Press, 1961), 321–28.

The editorial staff of *Conscience Africaine* has devoted many of its meetings to studying the difficult problems of the future of the Congo.

We are only a small group, but we think we can speak in the name of many because we have voluntarily limited ourselves to delivering and giving form to the aspirations and sentiments of the majority of thinking Congolese.

We have done this in a spirit of sincerity and with a desire to produce a constructive piece of work. What is more, we do not lay claim to any monopoly either of the love of our country or of clairvoyance for her future.

The present manifesto is only a point of departure. We will sharpen and complete it together with those who come later to join us.

Our National Vocation

In the history of the Congo, the last eighty years have been more important than the millenniums which have preceded them. The next thirty years will be decisive for our future. It would be vain to base our national sentiment on attachment to the past. It is toward the future that we turn our attention.

We believe that the Congo is called upon to become a great nation in the center of the African continent.

Our national vocation: to work in the heart of Africa to establish a new, prosperous, and happy society on the foundations of ancient clan society which has been vigorously shaken by too rapid an evolution, and which now seeks its new equilibrium.

We will only find this new equilibrium in the synthesis of our African character and temperament with the fundamental riches of Western civilization.

Only the Congolese, with the brotherly assistance of the Western people living in the Congo, can realize this synthesis.

In order to speak of a Congolese nation composed of Africans and Europeans, it is necessary that all be filled with the desire to serve the Congo. We have a right to demand of those Europeans who share in our national life to be, above all, Congolese citizens—that is to say, not to pursue only the good of the Belgian community and their own personal interests in the Congo, but to seek, together with us, the good of the great Congolese community.

A Noble Task to Pursue

Out of Belgium's civilizing actions in the Congo will develop a new civilization which will be ours. Already the principal elements of Western civilization are penetrating the Congo more and more intensely. Elementary education is reaching the masses, while an intellectual elite pursues its university study. The unceasing progress of science and technology struggles against illness and misery and establishes the foundations for a growing prosperity. The Christian religion teaches us the profound meaning of life, the eminent dignity of the human being, and the brotherhood of all men.

But we are still only half way—we want a complete civilization. An increasing number of Congolese want to take more responsibility and more initiative in the future of their country. They wish to assimilate in their national life other basic values of Western civilization which are still absent or insufficiently developed: respect for the individual and for his fundamental liberties without racial distinction; a more intense pursuit of social justice; a true democracy based on the equality of all men, and the participation of the people in the government of their country.

This is a long-term program which can be accomplished through the union of Africans and Europeans living in the Congo.

Belgo-Congolese Community?[1]

We state as fact that Congolese public opinion reacts with a certain distrust when one speaks of a "Belgo-Congolese Community." These words can cover very different realities.

To put it more clearly, the Congolese who reflect on these problems fear that some people distort the idea of the Belgo-Congolese community in order to put a brake on the total emancipation of the Congolese and to perpetuate indefinitely the European's domination, or at least preponderant influence, and thus form a privileged caste.

In the sense that we interpret it, such a community, far from being an obstacle, must be the means by which we realize our total emancipation.

For us the vision evoked by Governor General Pétillon is only an ideal of which we dream for the Congolese nation of tomorrow:

---

[1] In July 1955, the senior Belgian official in charge of the Congo, Governor-General Léon Pétillon, proposed in a speech to the colony's Government Council that a "Belgo-Congolese Community" needed to be envisioned to guarantee that the two countries would be associated "in perpetuity."

A human fraternity based on the fundamental equality of men without racial distinction.

Progressive But Total Emancipation

Belgium must not consider that there is a feeling of hostility in our desire for emancipation. Quite to the contrary, Belgium should be proud that, unlike nearly all colonized people, our desire is expressed without hatred or resentment. This alone is undeniable proof that the work of the Belgians in this country is not a failure.

If Belgium succeeds in leading the Congo to total emancipation intelligently and peacefully, it will be the first example in history of a colonial venture ending in complete success.

But to achieve that the Belgians must realize now that their domination of the Congo will not go on forever. We protest strongly against the opinion sometimes expressed in the press that does not make an essential distinction between the *presence* of the Belgians in the Congo and *their domination* of the Congo.

To those who ask: How long before the Belgians must leave the Congo?, we answer: Why do certain Belgians pose the question either dominate or abandon completely?

To those who pose this question, we would like to propose for the good both of the Congo and of the Belgians in the Congo, that they pack their bags without further delay.

It is time that the European elite react vigorously here in the Congo, and perhaps still more in Belgium, against such a dangerous mentality.

Whose fault is it if already too many Congolese are sure that the Europeans will not be able to abandon their attitude of political domination, economic exploitation, and racial superiority?

Political Emancipation

We have read that there is a question of a thirty-year plan for the political emancipation of the Congo. Without declaring ourselves on the whole of its component parts, we believe that such a plan has become a necessity if it is the intention to realize emancipation in peace and concord.

This plan should express the sincere will of Belgium to lead the Congo to its complete political emancipation in a period of thirty years.

Only an unequivocal declaration on this point will preserve the confidence of the Congolese toward Belgium. . . .

Order and Respect for Authority

It is our intention that the Congo's emancipation will be realized in order and tranquility. And we believe that it is possible.

We have decided not to let ourselves be drawn into violence, because violence produces insoluble problems. We have only one aim: the good of the Congolese nation. We will make this aim triumphant in lawfulness and by peaceful means. Those who use violence show that they are not ripe for true democracy.

We wish to continue to respect authority, but we want our opinion to be asked more than in the past; we want it given consideration, and if it is deemed impossible to follow us, we want to be told why.

We ask specially to be directly concerned, in the most formal way, in the elaboration of the contemplated thirty-year plan. Without this participation, such a plan could not have our assent. . . .

Need for the National Union

We have only one chance to make our cause triumphant: that is to be and to remain united.

United we will be strong, divided we will be weak; it is the future of the nation which is at stake.

National union is necessary because the whole population of the Congo must, before all else, be conscious of its national character and its unity. How will this be possible if the people are wooed by several competing parties?

But above all we do not want parties at present because what characterizes parties is conflict, while what we want is union.

If we let ourselves be divided, we will never realize the ideal of a great Congolese nation. Even if certain parties include political emancipation in their program, the mere existence of these parties is a radical obstacle to this emancipation.

Those Congolese who would be tempted to let themselves get drawn into party politics do not realize the old adage adopted by all dominators: "Divide and conquer"—To divide in order to dominate better.

29

ABAKO

Counter Manifesto for Belgian Congo

August 23, 1956

A few weeks after the Conscience Africaine *Manifesto appeared (see Document 28), the Alliance of the Bakongo, or ABAKO, presented its Counter Manifesto, proclaimed before an enormous crowd in the Belgian Congo capital of Léopoldville (now Kinshasa). The group then distributed the document throughout the country. ABAKO was founded in 1951 as a group interested in culture and language but emerged after 1954 as the colony's first non-European political organization. Its response to the Manifesto allowed it to affirm its political nature and goals. In 1957, ABAKO became a political party, sweeping elections in the colonial capital, and its members played a central role in Congolese politics through independence (1960). The excerpts here make clear the fundamental role that immediate emancipation played in the Counter Manifesto. It is interesting to note, however, that when it was first read aloud, newspaper reports indicate, speakers used the word "independence" in places where the text reads "emancipation." What also stands in contrast to the Manifesto is the important role politics played in the Counter Manifesto and the clear role its authors saw for the state regarding economic and social questions.*

1. Political Questions

. . .

B. THIRTY-YEAR PLAN

With respect to this plan, our friends from *Conscience Africaine* declare: "We ask specially to be directly concerned, in the most formal way, in the elaboration of the contemplated thirty-year plan. Without this participation, such a plan could not have our consent."

From Alan P. Merriam, *Congo: Background to Conflict* (Chicago: Northwestern University Press, 1961), 332–35.

For our part, we do not wish to collaborate in the elaboration of this plan but rather purely and simply to annul it because its application would serve only further to retard the Congo. In reality it is only the same old lullaby. Our patience is already exhausted. Since the hour has come, emancipation should be granted us this very day rather than delayed for another thirty years. History has never known delayed emancipations because when the hour has come people do not wait. If there is hesitation, it is no longer emancipation which terminates the crisis; it is hatred, revolt, separation, says Monsieur P. Ryekmans in his book, *Dominate to Serve*.

C. CONGOLESE UNION

Earlier we said that it is purely utopian to want to rally all the Congolese to one same opinion. The author of the thirty-year plan for the political emancipation of Belgian Africa recommends a Congolese Federation. We believe that he is on the right path. Considering the principle from Rousseau that "all which is not in nature has its drawbacks," and since the true union of the Congolese people can only be realized by way of political evolution, this evolution in the sense of democratic progress must begin first on an existing foundation. That means that groups historically, ethnically, and linguistically united or allied organize themselves to form as many political parties. Each "party" would elect its representatives. As in all democratic countries, the number of representatives would be in proportion to the population represented. A percentage would be determined; for example: one representative for 100,000 inhabitants. Only those elected will be able to bring about union and to trace the program of true democratization of the country. . . .

D. BELGO-CONGOLESE COMMUNITY

The problem which seems to preoccupy the Belgian politicans most at this time is that "of the institutional bonds with equal representation, between Belgium and the Congo" in the case where the latter had just gained its emancipation. What is our attitude? We espouse the opinion that the authors of the Manifesto have expressed. In effect, before thinking of the foundation of such a community, the Belgians ought to realize that it must be neither solicited nor imposed but freely chosen and accepted; they ought not to lose sight of the fact that the aims of the founder of their "domain" did not extend to the creation of a colony in the Congo but rather "to the organization of a Negro State.". . .

A caricature of the community copied from the famous French Union is not at all plausible for us; it is only a modified form of domination. Is it possible to conceive how this Congo, eighty times larger than Belgium, could become its "tenth province"? Would Belgium be able to tolerate having the inhabitants of her "tenth province" form the majority of the representatives in the Chamber? Perhaps a Commonwealth of the British pattern would be desirable.

2. Social and Economic Questions

. . .

. . . The largest Congolese companies forget their duties and substitute themselves for the state and the unions, and sometimes even for the press. What they call social works are in reality only a reinvestment of profits, a budgetary balance, a refining of the calculations. We know how to build hospitals, schools, foyers where they are not even necessary; we know how to construct city gardens, but we do not dare to add one cent to the salary of the unhappy Negro for fear that the treasury would be ruined. Obviously, one would have to be a fool not to understand that these social works have a purely political end; they constitute "a museum" to distract the tourists and to deceive the visitors of note.

Nationalization of the large business enterprises would be desirable for the parastatals [businesses partially owned by the Belgian state], as well as for the large mineral and agricultural companies, in order to permit the state to fulfill the new needs which have proved increasingly important and complicated.

B. AFRICANIZATION OF THE STAFFS

There is talk these days in A.E.F. [French Equatorial Africa] of an Africanization of staffs. We think that it is also the moment to reflect on the "Congolization" of staffs in the Administration as well as in private business enterprises. Here again, the lack of university elite must not serve as a pretext for wanting to find a place for the Negroes on lower staffs. Sometimes it is only the color bar, pure jealousy. What places are occupied by the graduates of the school of Administration at Kisantu? Where do those from St. Luke's school of art go? Aren't the medical assistants comparable to the mere sanitary agents from Europe?

We do not ask for such offices as those which have fallen to our well-known city chief in Léopoldville, where the Negro is only an emblem—offices which some shrewd person invented with the unique political aim of falsifying world opinion—but true offices where the Negro assumes real responsibilities with all the usual latitude of the offices. Besides, if we are lacking an elite, it is for them, the Belgians, to confess the fault, as was shown so clearly by Monsieur Van Bilsen when he declared: "It is our fault, not theirs, if among the Negroes there are neither doctors, nor engineers, nor civil servants, nor officers. The Missionaries have, in their own field of action, trained hundreds of priests one of whom has already received Episcopal sanction. In the Belgian Congo and in Ruanda-Urundi, the formation of elite groups and of responsible directing staffs is a generation behind the British colonial territories and the bordering colonies."

30

HAROLD MACMILLAN

"Wind of Change" Speech

February 3, 1960

Since 1910, the Union of South Africa had been a self-governing dominion, first within the British Empire and then within the British Commonwealth, which was established in 1931. In 1948, its government began to pursue a policy that came to be known as "apartheid," which aimed at complete separation of legally defined racial groups. One crucial implication was that South Africa was to be a state for "whites" only. Members of other groups— "natives" (or "blacks"), "Asians" (primarily people with origins in South Asia), and "coloreds" (people of mixed race) —were destined to have their own separate states. In 1961, faced with growing criticism from other members of the Commonwealth, South Africa became a republic and cut direct institutional ties with Great Britain.

The speech by Prime Minister Harold Macmillan excerpted here, made several months before South Africa's break with the United Kingdom, is often seen as the first public, albeit tacit, criticism by a British leader of the apartheid system. Given before South Africa's parliament, at the end of a month-long tour of African countries that had been British colonies

From *African Yearbook of Rhetoric* 2, no. 3 (2011): 29, 31–32.

(Ghana) or still were (e.g., Nigeria), the speech announced that Britain now accepted the decolonization of Africa. Note how Macmillan gives credit to British and European sources for developments that, until this speech, the British government had ardently opposed.

It is . . . a special privilege for me to be here in 1960 when you are celebrating what I might call the golden wedding of the Union [of South Africa, which was founded in 1910]. At such a time it is natural and right that you should pause to take stock of your position, to look back at what you have achieved, to look forward to what lies ahead. . . .

. . . As I've travelled around the Union I have found everywhere, as I expected, a deep preoccupation with what is happening in the rest of the African continent. I understand and sympathise with your interests in these events and your anxiety about them. Ever since the break-up of the Roman empire one of the constant facts of political life in Europe has been the emergence of independent nations. They have come into existence over the centuries in different forms, different kinds of government, but all have been inspired by a deep, keen feeling of nationalism, which has grown as the nations have grown.

In the twentieth century, and especially since the end of the war [1945], the processes which gave birth to the nation states of Europe have been repeated all over the world. We have seen the awakening of national consciousness in peoples who have for centuries lived in dependence upon some other power. Fifteen years ago this movement spread through Asia. Many countries there, of different races and civilisations, pressed their claim to an independent national life. Today the same thing is happening in Africa, and the most striking of all the impressions I have formed since I left London a month ago is of the strength of this African national consciousness. In different places it takes different forms, but it is happening everywhere. The wind of change is blowing through this continent, and whether we like it or not, this growth of national consciousness is a political fact. We must all accept it as a fact, and our national policies must take account of it.

Of course you understand this better than anyone, you are sprung from Europe, the home of nationalism, here in Africa you have yourselves created a free nation. A new nation. Indeed in the history of our times yours will be recorded as the first of the African nationalists. This tide of national consciousness which is now rising in Africa, is a fact, for which both you and we, and the other nations of the western world are ultimately responsible. For its causes are to be found in the achievements of western civilisation, in the pushing forward of the frontiers of knowledge, the applying of science to the service of human needs, in the expanding of food production, in the speeding and multiplying of the means of communication, and perhaps above all and more than anything else in the spread of education.

As I have said, the growth of national consciousness in Africa is a political fact, and we must accept it as such. That means, I would judge, that we've got to come to terms with it. I sincerely believe that if we cannot do so we may imperil the precarious balance between the East and West on which the peace of the world depends.

The world today is divided into three main groups. First there are what we call the Western Powers. You in South Africa and we in Britain belong to this group, together with our friends and allies in other parts of the Commonwealth. In the United States of America and in Europe we call it the Free World. Secondly there are the Communists—Russia, her satellites in Europe, China whose population will rise by the end of the next ten years to the staggering total of 800 million. And then thirdly, there are those parts of the world whose people are at present uncommitted either to Communism or to our Western ideas.

And in this context we think first of Asia and then of Africa. As I see it the great issue in this second half of the twentieth century is whether the uncommitted peoples of Asia and Africa will swing to the East or to the West. Will they be drawn into the Communist camp? Or will the great experiments in self-government that are now being made in Asia and Africa, especially within the Commonwealth, prove so successful, and by their example so compelling, that the balance will come down in favour of freedom and order and justice?

The struggle is joined, and it is a struggle for the minds of men. What is now on trial is much more than our military strength or our diplomatic and administrative skill. It is our way of life. The uncommitted nations want to see before they choose.

31

INGRID JONKER

The Child Who Was Shot Dead by Soldiers at Nyanga

1960

The situation in South Africa, a formally independent country governed under the principles of apartheid (1948–1991), was a widely debated topic in the context of the era of decolonization and after. Those who fought to overturn the apartheid system constantly compared South Africa to other European colonies. This was the case, for example, with Nelson Mandela, who was imprisoned in 1964 because of his leadership of Umkhonto we Sizwe, the armed wing of the African National Congress. The defenders of apartheid insisted that the white people of South Africa—both those who spoke Afrikaans, a language with Dutch roots that had developed there, and those who spoke English—were also indigenous to the country and had the right to protect their white culture. To this end, South African laws sought to exclude all nonwhites from any rights whatsoever. One of the symbols of these efforts was the Pass Laws, which required nonwhites to carry a document indicating their racial status and limiting their movements. These laws inspired growing protests during the late 1950s and early 1960s. The most well-known protest was in the poor black-only township of Sharpeville in early 1960, when the police opened fire on protesters and killed sixty-nine young people.

Ingrid Jonker, a young Afrikaans-speaking white woman, wrote this poem in response to another police shooting in early 1960, in Nyanga, a township near Cape Town. The poem's invocation of "Afrika" was taken by many people to mean that Jonker saw what was happening as part of a continent-wide struggle. Jonker committed suicide before her poem was published. Nelson Mandela chose to read it in the original Afrikaans on May 24, 1994, when he spoke at the opening of the first post-apartheid democratic parliament.

Poem translated by Jack Cope in Ann Harries, Roger Diski, and Alasdair Brown, *The Child Is Not Dead: Youth Resistance in South Africa, 1976–86* (London: British Defence and Aid Fund for Southern Africa, 1986), 12.

The child is not dead
the child lifts his fists against his mother
who shouts Afrika! shouts the breath
of freedom and the veld
in the locations of the cordoned heart

The child lifts his fists against his father
in the march of the generations
who are shouting Afrika! shout the breath
of righteousness and blood
in the streets of his embattled pride

The child is not dead
not at Langa nor at Nyanga
not at Orlando nor at Sharpeville
nor at the police station at Philippi
where he lies with a bullet through his brain

The child is the dark shadow of the soldiers
on guard with their rifles, saracens [armored cars] and batons
the child is present at all assemblies and law-giving
the child peers through the windows of houses and into the hearts
    of mothers
this child who wanted only to play in the sun at Nyanga is everywhere
the child grown to a man treks through all Africa
the child grown into a giant journeys over the whole world

Without a pass

32

UNITED NATIONS GENERAL ASSEMBLY

Declaration on the Granting of Independence to Colonial Countries and Peoples

December 14, 1960

The United Nations was established in 1945 to maintain peace among existing states. Its crucial decision-making body, the Security Council, gave exceptional privileges to five great powers, which included the two European states with the largest overseas empires, France and the United Kingdom, along with China, the Soviet Union, and the United States. The eloquent preamble to the UN Charter (see Document 2) came from the pen of South African prime minister Jan Smuts, a dedicated imperialist and racist. Yet the United Nations slowly became a forum that met the hopes of anticolonialists. This was largely because a growing number of previously colonized states joined it and transformed the General Assembly, which became a bully pulpit to condemn colonialism.

In 1960, nineteen new states were admitted, and they catalyzed the emergence of a new majority within the organization. In the midst of the cold war, these states affirmed that they were uncommitted to either side; as such, they were variously termed the nonaligned bloc, the Bandung group, the developing world, or the third world. This informal majority came into view when its members drafted the stirring Declaration on the Granting of Independence to Colonial Countries and Peoples, which their diplomats succeeded in bringing to a vote, despite intense opposition from the Western powers. No country, however, voted against it, and its adoption sharply shifted the UN's stance on empire. Unlike the original charter, it celebrated national independence, with the implication that no other freedom was possible without it.

The General Assembly:
    Mindful of the determination proclaimed by the peoples of the world in the Charter of the United Nations to reaffirm faith in fundamental

From John Allphin Moore Jr. and Jerry Pubantz, *Encyclopedia of the United Nations*, 2nd ed. (New York: Facts On File, 2007), 1:106–7.

HUMAN RIGHTS, in the dignity and worth of the human person, in the equal rights of men and WOMEN and of nations large and small and to promote social progress and better standards of life in larger freedom,

Conscious of the need for the creation of conditions of stability and well-being and peaceful and friendly relations based on respect for the principles of equal rights and self-determination of all peoples, and of universal respect for, and observance of, human rights and fundamental freedoms for all without distinction as to race, sex, language or religion,

Recognizing the passionate yearning for freedom in all dependent peoples and the decisive role of such peoples in the attainment of their independence,

Aware of the increasing conflicts resulting from the denial of or impediments in the way of the freedom of such peoples, which constitute a serious threat to world peace,

Considering the important role of the United Nations in assisting the movement for independence in Trust and NON-SELF-GOVERNING TERRITORIES,

Recognizing that the peoples of the world ardently desire the end of colonialism in all its manifestations,

Convinced that the continued existence of colonialism prevents the development of international economic co-operation, impedes the social, cultural and economic DEVELOPMENT of dependent peoples and militates against the United Nations ideal of universal peace,

Affirming that peoples may, for their own ends, freely dispose of their natural wealth and resources without prejudice to any obligations arising out of international economic co-operation, based upon the principle of mutual benefit, and INTERNATIONAL LAW,

Believing that the process of liberation is irresistible and irreversible and that, in order to avoid serious crises, an end must be put to colonialism and all practices of segregation and discrimination associated therewith,

Welcoming the emergence in recent years of a large number of dependent territories into freedom and independence, and recognizing the increasingly powerful trends towards freedom in such territories which have not yet attained independence,

Convinced that all peoples have an inalienable right to complete freedom, the exercise of their SOVEREIGNTY and the integrity of their national territory,

Solemnly proclaims the necessity of bringing to a speedy and unconditional end colonialism in all its forms and manifestations;

And to this end

Declares that:

1. The subjection of peoples to alien subjugation, domination and exploitation constitutes a denial of fundamental human rights, is contrary to the Charter of the United Nations and is an impediment to the promotion of world peace and co-operation.

2. All peoples have the right to self-determination; by virtue of that right they freely determine their political status and freely pursue their economic, social and cultural development.

3. Inadequacy of political, economic, social or educational preparedness should never serve as a pretext for delaying independence.

4. All armed action or repressive measures of all kinds directed against dependent peoples shall cease in order to enable them to exercise peacefully and freely their right to complete independence, and the integrity of their national territory shall be respected.

5. Immediate steps shall be taken, in Trust and Non-Self-Governing Territories or all other territories which have not yet attained independence, to transfer all powers to the peoples of those territories, without any conditions or reservations, in accordance with their freely expressed will and desire, without any distinction as to race, creed or colour, in order to enable them to enjoy complete independence and freedom.

6. Any attempt aimed at the partial or total disruption of the national unity and the territorial integrity of a country is incompatible with the purposes and principles of the Charter of the United Nations.

7. All States shall observe faithfully and strictly the provisions of the Charter of the United Nations, the UNIVERSAL DECLARATION OF HUMAN RIGHTS and the present Declaration on the basis of equality, non-interference in the internal affairs of all States, and respect for the sovereign rights of all peoples and their territorial integrity.

33

ALVIM PEREIRA

Ten Principles

1961

Portugal's empire remained intact as other European overseas empires ended. Unlike Belgium, the Netherlands, France, and the United Kingdom, which witnessed, to varying degrees, a postwar economic boom and withdrew from their most significant overseas colonies by 1963, Portugal remained starkly poor and underdeveloped, governed by an undemocratic regime that held on to its colonies. It was not until 1975 that Portugal's most important African colonies, Angola and Mozambique, gained independence. The precipitating factor was the April 1974 nonviolent revolution in the metropole, called the Carnation Revolution. In an incredible irony, the group of army colonels who overthrew the authoritarian government modeled their movement on African anticolonial groups whom the Portuguese had been fighting since the 1960s; some described listening to rebel radio broadcasts in the bush and learning from what they heard. The arguments of Amilcar Cabral (see Document 35), who had led Guinea-Bissau to freedom in 1973, were particularly important.

Until the revolution, the Portuguese government had been a vocal critic of all anticolonial movements, energetically intervening in the UN and other public forums to defend European overseas empires in general and their own in particular. The following document was distributed by a Portuguese archbishop, Alvim Pereira, to seminarians and priests in his archdiocese. Pereira's "Ten Principles" survives thanks to the efforts of several of the African seminarians, who were shocked by its contents. It offers a clear statement of the anti-Communist and pro-Catholic arguments on which the Portuguese government relied. It also provides an interesting depiction of the complicated role the Roman Catholic Church played across the world during the era of decolonization.

Translation by Gabriel Paquette from a copy of the original document, which Dr. Luis B. Serapião kindly made available from his personal papers.

1. Independence has no bearing on the welfare of man. It can be good if the right conditions are present (the cultural conditions do not yet exist in Mozambique).
2. In the absence of such conditions, to found or take part in movements that seek independence is to act against nature.
3. Even if these conditions existed, the Metropole has the right to oppose independence so long as the freedoms and rights of man are respected, and [the Metropole] seeks to secure access to well-being as well as civil and religious progress to all people.
4. All movements which use force (terrorists) violate natural law, because independence, if it is to be assumed a positive development, must result from peaceful means.
5. When the movement is a terrorist one, the clergy have the obligation, in good conscience, not only to refrain from taking part, but also to oppose it. This [obligation] derives from the nature of his mission [as a religious leader].
6. Even when the movement is peaceful, the clergy must not participate in order to remain the spiritual guide of all people. The bishop of the church may impose that abstention; he imposes it now for Lourenço Marques [the capital of Mozambique, now named Maputo].
7. The native people of Africa should recognize all the benefits that the colonizers have given them.
8. The educated have the duty to combat the illusions about independence held by the less educated.
9. The present African independence movements, almost all of them, were born under the sign of Revolution and Communism. The doctrine of the Holy See is quite clear in its opposition to atheistic and revolutionary Communism. The great revolution is that of the Gospel.
10. The slogan "Africa for the Africans" is a philosophical monstrosity and a challenge to the Christian civilization, because current events tell us that it is Communism and Islam which wish to impose their civilization upon the Africans. Another way to say this would be: "Africa for the Russians and Asians."

34

CELINA SIMANGO

Speech at the International Women's Congress in Moscow

June 1963

In June 1962, a diverse group of Mozambican men and women who sought immediate independence for their homeland founded the Mozambique Liberation Front (FRELIMO). Some were religious leaders, while others were committed leftists. FRELIMO's ideology was an inchoate mix of leftist calls for social equality and modernization along with critiques of capitalism and traditionalism. Notably, some members insisted that the fights against racism and sexism were as important as addressing the economic questions.

Two women led efforts to target the colonial and traditional structures that, they claimed, produced sexism. Janet Mondlane, a white American who was married to the first president of FRELIMO, Eduardo Mondlane, played a crucial role in the movement. She became the head of the Mozambique Institute, which had oversight over the movement's educational activities. Celina Simango, who became a leader of FRELIMO's League of Mozambican Women, was the wife of a Presbyterian pastor, Uria Simango, who became FRELIMO's first vice president. The Simangos were critical of the influence of Marxism in the movement.

The following excerpts are from a June 1963 speech by Celina Simango at the Fifth International Women's Congress, which took place in Moscow and involved close to 2,000 delegates from 119 countries. They originally appeared in Mozambican Revolution, *an English-language publication from FRELIMO. The Soviets treated the congress as a propaganda tool to present themselves as defenders of women's rights. The attendant international publicity offered anticolonial women's groups an opportunity to introduce their concerns on the world stage.*

From *Mozambican Revolution*, no. 1 (December 1963): 10.

First of all I wish to thank the Women's International [Democratic] Federation[1] for inviting me to represent the Women of Mozambique in this Congress. My country is one of the least known in Africa, if only because we had the misfortune of being controlled by Portuguese imperialism for many centuries. Therefore, before discussing the subject at hand I would like to tell you a little about my country and my people. . . .

The whole economy of our country is geared towards the satisfaction of the European settlers. In order to make certain that the European settlers get the fullest economic advantage from the African worker, the Portuguese government has used many techniques of forcing our people to work in European farms, industries and commercial enterprises, mostly in menial jobs. . . . The women and younger people are also forced to work in European plantations within Mozambique.

. . . If any women in the whole world should understand the need for peace, it is the African women in general and the Mozambican women in particular. As an African woman I am extremely aware of the need for peace partly because Africa has not yet known peace for the last one hundred years. Since the European imperialist parcelled our continent into enclaves of European capitalist exploitation, they have been taking away the best of our men to feed their economic enterprises with cheap labor, while leaving the women and children behind to fend for existence in the poorest conditions. . . . We however give our complete support to the worthy efforts of the women of our free sister states in the rest of Africa, who are relentlessly putting pressure on the major powers to achieve a workable scheme for disarmament. . . . All of the problem and difficulties which our people are facing in Mozambique cannot be changed simply by condemning them. No moralizing against the colonialists is sufficient to get rid of the situation we are facing. . . . Therefore, the people of Mozambique have decided to fight for their freedom.

[1] The Women's International Democratic Federation (WIDF) was founded in Paris in 1945. It had four priorities: antifascism, international peace, child welfare, and the status of women. While the organization was nonpartisan, numerous Communist party members were involved. In the United States, the House Un-American Activities Committee (HUAC) investigated the U.S. branch in 1949 and charged that it served Soviet interests. The U.S. branch left the WIDF months later.

35

AMILCAR CABRAL

Anonymous Soldiers for the United Nations

December 12, 1962

With the 1960 Declaration on the Granting of Independence to Colonial Countries and Peoples (see Document 32), the United Nations became a beacon for anticolonialists. One who came to the organization seeking support was a young agricultural engineer born in Cape Verde (then a Portuguese island colony off the west coast of Africa) and trained in Portuguese universities. Amilcar Cabral used the audience he obtained before the Fourth Committee of the UN General Assembly in New York to publicize the existence and demands of his political party, the African Party for the Independence of Guinea and Cape Verde (PAIGC, the initials of its Portuguese name). Along with the public declaration excerpted here, he submitted a massive report purporting to show that according to the UN Charter and UN resolutions, Portugal had no legal right to rule its overseas colonies. The UN chose not to act on this claim, and the PAIGC became known for its armed struggle against Portuguese rule. It was the first armed movement that succeeded in forcing the end of colonial rule in sub-Saharan Africa, with Guinean independence declared in 1973. Cabral himself was assassinated shortly thereafter by disgruntled PAIGC rivals. In this excerpt, note how Cabral pivots from the letter of international law to its spirit, which allows him to affirm the legitimacy of armed struggle in the name of national independence.

The UN resolution on decolonialisation has created a new situation for our struggle. Having been condemned, the colonial system, whose immediate and total elimination is demanded by this resolution, is now an international crime. We have thus obtained a legal basis for demanding the elimination of the colonial yoke in our country and for using all necessary means to destroy that yoke. But this applies not only to us.

From Amilcar Cabral, *Revolution in Guinea, Stage 1* (New York: Monthly Review Press, 1974), 50–52.

On the basis of the resolution, the United Nations and the anti-colonialist states and organizations—all the forces of peace in the world—can and must take concrete action against the Portuguese state. Illegally and against the interests of civilisation, the Portuguese state is continuing to perpetrate both in our country and in other African countries the "crime of colonialisation," thus endangering international peace and security.

We are certain that the Portuguese government cannot persist with impunity in committing an international crime. We are also certain that the United Nations has at its disposal all the means necessary to conceive and carry out concrete and effective measures both to make the principles of the Charter be respected and to impose international legality in our countries and to defend the interests of peace and of civilisation.

We are not here to ask the UN to send troops to free our countries from the Portuguese colonial yoke. Perhaps we could ask for it, but we do not think it necessary, for we are confident that we will be able to free our countries. We invoke only one right: the right to obtain collaboration and concrete assistance from the UN in order to hasten the liberation of our countries from the colonial yoke and thus to lessen the human and material losses which a long struggle can cause.

Our struggle has lost its strictly national character and has moved onto an international level. The struggle taking place in our country today is the struggle of progress against misery and suffering, of freedom against oppression. While it is true that the victims of this struggle are none other than the children of our people, it is nevertheless true that each of our comrades who dies under torture or falls under the fire of the Portuguese colonialist machine-guns identifies himself, through the hopes and certainties which we all carry in our hearts and minds, with all men who love peace and freedom and wish to live a life of progress and happiness.

We are not just fighting for the realisation of our aspirations to freedom and national independence. We are fighting—and will fight until final victory—so that the resolutions and the Charter of the United Nations will be respected. In the prisons, in the towns and in the countryside of our land the battle is being fought today between the UN, which demands the elimination of the colonial system of domination of peoples, and the armed forces of the Portuguese government, which wishes to perpetuate this system against the legitimate rights of our people.

Who are we in fact, waging this struggle against the Portuguese colonialists in particularly difficult conditions?

When in Elizabethville [a large Congolese city] or in the Congo bush a soldier of Indian, Ethiopian or other nationality falls under the fire of the enemy, he is one more victim who has given his life for the cause of the UN. He dies for a just ideal, since he believes that the UN resolutions on the Congo were aimed at achieving unity, peace and progress for the Congolese people in the independence which they reconquered and to which they have a right.

To have its resolutions respected, the UN has mobilised soldiers, pilots, administrators, technicians and experts of all sorts, and is spending enormous sums each day.

When in our country a comrade dies under police torture, is assassinated in prison, is burned alive or falls under the bullets of Portuguese guns, for which cause is he giving his life?

He is giving it for the liberation of our people from the colonial yoke, and hence for the UN. In fighting and dying for the liberation of our countries we are giving our lives, in the present context of international legality, for the ideal which the UN itself has defined in its Charter, in its resolutions, and in particular in its resolution on decolonialisation.

For us, the only difference between the Indian soldier, the Italian pilot or the Swedish administrator who dies in the Congo and our comrade who dies in Guinea or the Cabo [Cape] Verde Islands is that by acting in our country for the same ideal we are simply *anonymous soldiers for the UN.*

The names of our comrades who have fallen victims of the Portuguese colonialists are not on the files of the UN. We have never been paid or equipped by the UN, nor do we have any budget assigned to cover the ever-increasing costs of our struggle. But in the uneven struggle which we are forced to wage we are nonetheless at the service of the UN, defending its prestige and the respect owed by all governments to the resolutions of an international character which it has adopted.

36

ZHOU ENLAI

Conversation with S. V. Chervonenko

April 20, 1965

The intersecting histories of decolonization and the cold war gave rise
to many questions. Among the most important was how overseas European imperialism differed from other forms of colonialism and whether
countries without a formal empire could be imperialist. Both the Soviet
Union and the United States faced accusations throughout the era that
they were, in practice, imperialist powers. For the Soviets, the breakup of
their country in the early 1990s, which saw the supposedly willing member republics all declare independence, offers clear evidence for claims
that even if it was land based and loudly anti-imperialist, the USSR was
an empire. For the United States, its participation in the Vietnam War
(1961–1975) made it an easy target for those who wanted to extend the
lessons they had learned from anticolonialism to other forms of international power politics.

    The following selection suggests how Communist leaders drew inspi-
ration from anticolonial struggles to critique U.S. actions, such as its
growing involvement in South Vietnam, which the Americans claimed
were in defense of freedom and against Communist domination. It must
also be read, however, as an element of already fraught and still growing
tensions between the Soviets and the Chinese Communists. These difficulties had burst into public view in 1959 and 1960, and culminated in a
clear split between Moscow and Beijing in 1961. Led by Mao Zedong,
founder of the People's Republic of China (PRC), the Chinese used their
role as a non-European and third world power, which had been on
display at Bandung in 1955, as one aspect of their larger claim that they
were truly revolutionary and Marxist, in opposition to the "revisionist"
USSR.

    On April 13, 1965, Chinese premier Zhou Enlai invited Soviet ambas-
sador to the PRC S. V. Chervonenko to a dinner in connection with the
forthcoming departure of the ambassador for his homeland. Zhou, on his

"Conversation between Soviet Ambassador to China, S. V. Chervonenko and Chinese
Prime Minister, Zhou Enlai (Fragment)," Wilson Center, Digital Archive, http://
digitalarchive.wilsoncenter.org/document/112454.

own initiative, started a conversation that continued for over two hours. The following is an excerpt of Zhou's remarks during that discussion. Note his reference to Ahmed Ben Bella, the first president of the Algerian republic. Both the Chinese and the Soviets wanted his support, with the Chinese particularly eager to get Algerian backing for their claim that China represented the third world.

In some countries, where I visited, the intensity of struggle in Vietnam, the heroism and decisiveness of the Vietnamese people in the struggle, are not clearly appreciated. Therefore we consider it useful to make visits, which offer an opportunity to talk about these events, to tell about events.

Let's take Algiers, for example. After all, the Algerians themselves came to a victory as a result of a prolonged struggle against the French aggressors. Algerians are also concerned about the struggle of the Vietnamese people against American imperialism, they can envision the possibility that the Americans could suppress the struggle of the Vietnamese people. The Algerians' concern is also caused by the fact that they can envision the possibility that the [North] Vietnamese could opt for talks in the face of bombardment. When we were in Algiers we told the Algerians that the situation in South Vietnam now is the same as it once was in Algiers. After all, the Algerians also fought against an 800,000 strong army of the French colonialists, but were not intimidated by them. But in Vietnam the population is higher than in Algiers. In South Vietnam alone the population is 14 million, and in North Vietnam— 17 million. Thus, Vietnam's population on the whole exceeds 30 million people. To this one must add that the Vietnamese are fully determined to struggle against the aggression. After our explanation the Algerians began to understand more clearly the situation in Vietnam.

We also informed the Algerians, that now in South Vietnam the numbers of regular and semi-regular armies on the whole do not exceed 500,000 people. And there are about 30 thousand American soldiers there now. When I spoke to Ben Bella I told him that their number is only slightly higher than 20 thousand. The South Vietnamese hold the American aggressors in disdain, they will continue the struggle, even if new [U.S.] forces arrive in South Vietnam.

Recently President Ho Chi Minh said that even if there were several tens of thousands of American soldiers in South Vietnam, the struggle would have to be continued, and the war brought to the end.

We also gave another example. During the war in Algeria, some members of the provisional government stood for compromise, for negotiations, but the majority in the leadership spoke for resistance, for taking the struggle to the end. And then, as a result of that part of the leadership prevailing, after 7 years of war Algerians entered into negotiations and won a victory. If during the first period of the war in Algeria, those who stood for agreement-making, for compromise, would have prevailed, then the victory would not have been achieved. The victory in Algeria was achieved precisely thanks to the present Algerian leadership. This question is absolutely clear.

When I was in Algiers last time, Ben Bella himself talked about this. This time I told him that South Vietnam is at the stage of struggle in which the Algerian people found themselves several years ago. I suggested that Ben Bella think about the following question: before, they were under the yoke of the French aggressors; the Vietnamese people were also under the yoke of the French aggressors, and now they are under the yoke of American aggressors. How can the Vietnamese people not take the struggle against American aggressors to a victorious end? We also told the Algerians that, as the Vietnamese comrades think, if one is to opt for a compromise now, this would result in more victims than if one were to continue the struggle to the end. Once Ben Bella heard my explanations, he understood the situation in Vietnam and came to a conclusion that if the Vietnamese accepted a cease-fire and entered into negotiations, this would result in more victims in South Vietnam and South Vietnam would not achieve its independence.

37

FAYEZ A. SAYEGH

Zionist Colonialism in Palestine

1965

In the years after the establishment of the State of Israel, the hopes of politically active Palestinians focused primarily on Arab nationalism. Arab leaders such as Gamal Abdel Nasser in Egypt (see Document 14), as well as various nationalist groups in other Arab countries, promised that the unity of all Arab peoples would allow Israel to be beaten and all of Palestine to be reunited under Arab rule. Those few Palestinians who were ready to accept Israel as an independent Jewish state had counted on the international community for help. Yet although the United States and other Israeli allies repeatedly voted in favor of UN resolutions summoning Israel to repatriate the more than 700,000 Palestinian Arabs who had been expelled by or fled from Israeli troops in 1948, Israel did not comply.

By the early 1960s, some younger and more radical elements of the Palestinian nationalist movement argued that Palestinians could not wait any longer for help from fellow Arabs or from the international community. They had to take action. Two developments encouraged such thinking. The first was the 1961 secession of Syria from the United Arab Republic, which in 1958 had joined Egypt and Syria under the rule of Nasser. This made the realization of Arab unity seem far more difficult than previously imagined. The second was Algerian independence in 1962, which suggested that one Arab nation, on its own, could vanquish foreign domination, with or without Arab unity. By 1964, some forty different groups committed to fighting for Palestinian independence had emerged. The largest, the Palestinian National Liberation Movement, known as Fatah (an acronym of its Arabic name), was led by Yasir Arafat, who had trained with National Liberation Front forces in Morocco. Fatah began to conduct armed attacks on Israeli positions in 1965.

In early 1964, in response to growing Palestinian militancy, the Arab League (which linked together the leaders of independent Arab states) summoned a meeting of what it called the Palestinian National Council.

From Fayez A. Sayegh, *Zionist Colonialism in Palestine* (Beirut: Research Center, Palestine Liberation Organization, 1965), v–vi, 1–2, 11, 19, 49–52.

*It was at this meeting that the Palestine Liberation Organization (PLO)
was born. Its goal was the liberation of Palestine, which meant the establishment of one state comprising all of the territory of British Mandatory
Palestine, with no distinct Jewish state. The more radical groups, fearing
that the Arab leaders would use it to subordinate their fight for Palestinian independence to other goals, remained outside the PLO until 1968.*

*The following is an excerpt from the PLO's first official publication. Its
author, Fayez A. Sayegh, a U.S.-trained historian and Palestinian Christian, positions Palestinian demands in the context of anticolonialism and
modern European imperialism. Such arguments have long been central
to pro-Palestinian criticisms of Israel. By contrast, defenders of Israel usually insist that the post-1948 Arab-Israeli conflict needs to be understood
in the specific context of Jewish history, both the Bible's descriptions of the
land as Jewish and the long history of anti-Semitism, especially the Nazi-
engineered mass murder of some six million European Jews in the 1930s
and 1940s.*

Foreword

The past two decades, which have witnessed the collapse of European
Imperialism and the progressive elimination of Western Colonialism
from Asia and Africa, have witnessed also the introduction of a new form
of Colonialism into the point-of-intersection of those two continents.
Thus, the fading-out of a cruel and shameful period of world history
has coincided with the emergence, at the land-bridge between Asia and
Africa, of a new offshoot of European Imperialism and a new variety of
racist Colonialism.

The fate of Palestine thus represents an *anomaly*, a radical departure
from the trend of contemporary world history. Scores of nations and
peoples have come to enjoy their right to self-determination, at the very
time when the Arab people of Palestine was finding itself helpless to
prevent the culmination of a process of systematic colonization to which
Palestine had been subjected for decades. This climactic development
took the combined form of forcible dispossession of the indigenous population, their expulsion from their own country, the implantation of an
alien sovereignty on their soil, and the speedy importation of hordes of
aliens to occupy the land thus emptied of its rightful inhabitants.

The people of Palestine has lost not only *political control* over its
country, but *physical occupation* of its country as well: it has been

deprived not only of its inalienable right to *self-determination*, but also of its elemental right to exist on its own land!

This *dual* tragedy, which befell the Arab people of Palestine in the middle of the twentieth century, symbolize the *dual* nature of the Zionist program which had begun to unfold itself in Palestine in the late nineteenth century.

The Historical Setting of Zionist Colonialism

The frenzied "Scramble for Africa" of the 1880's stimulated the beginnings of Zionist colonization in Palestine. As European fortune-hunters, prospective settlers, and empire-builders raced for Africa, Zionist settlers and would-be state-builders rushed for Palestine.

Under the influence of the credo of Nationalism then sweeping across Europe, some Jews had come to believe that the religious and alleged racial bonds among Jews constituted a Jewish "nationality" and endowed the so-called "Jewish nation" with normal national rights including the right to *separate existence* in a territory of its own, and the right to create a Jewish *state*. If other European nations had successfully extended themselves into Asia and Africa, and had annexed to their imperial domains vast portions of those two continents, the "Jewish nation"—it was argued—was entitled and able to do the same thing for itself. By imitating the colonial ventures of the "Gentile [non-Jewish] nations" among whom Jews lived, the "Jewish nation" could send its own *colonists* into a piece of Afro-Asian territory, establish a *settler-community*, and, in due course, set up its own *state*—not, indeed, as an imperial outpost of a metropolitan home-base, but as a home-base in its own right, upon which the entire "Jewish nation" would sooner or later converge from all over the world. "Jewish nationalism" would thus fulfill itself through the process of colonization, which other European nations had utilized for empire-building. For Zionism, then, colonization would be the instrument of nation-building, not the by-product of an already-fulfilled nationalism. . . .

The Alliance of British Imperialism and Zionist Colonialism

. . . The Zionist settler-state remains *an alien body* in the region. Not only its vital and continuing association with European Imperialism, and its introduction into Palestine of the practices of Western Colonialism, but also its chosen pattern of racial exclusiveness and self-segregation renders it an alien society in the Middle East. No words could better describe the essentially alien character of the Zionist settler-state than the following passage, written by its veteran Prime Minister [David Ben-Gurion]:[1]

> The State of Israel is a part of the Middle East only in geography, which is, in the main, a static element. From the decisive aspects of dynamism, creation and growth, Israel is a part of world Jewry. From that Jewry it will draw all the strength and the means for the forging of the nation in Israel and the development of the Land; through the might of world Jewry it will be built and built again.[2] . . .

Epilogue: The Liberation of Palestine

. . . In its determination to pursue the difficult path of national liberation, the people of Palestine is encouraged by the faith in the justice of its cause repeatedly expressed by newly-liberated peoples in successive international conferences. From Bandung to Accra, from Casablanca[3] to Belgrade,[4] that faith in the justice of the cause of the Palestinian Arabs has been clearly expressed. And, at the Second Conference of the Heads of State or Government of Non-Aligned Countries, "full support to the Arab people of Palestine in their struggle for liberation from colonialism and racism" was solemnly declared. The supreme leaders of peoples who still retain vivid memories of their recent experiences under imperialism, colonialism, and/or racism have thus evinced responsiveness to the pains and hopes of the Palestinian people, still suffering from all these evils and from dispossession and dispersion as well. Such responsiveness cannot fail to augment the profound faith of Palestinians in the ultimate triumph of justice, liberty, and human dignity in their land.

The problem of Palestine, although it directly afflicts only the Palestinians, is not the concern of Palestinians alone.

The Zionist settler-state, bent on expansion, is a threat to the security and territorial integrity of *the Arab states* as well. It has already invaded their lands. It still covets their territories.

As a colonial venture, which anomalously came to bloom precisely when colonialism was beginning to fade away, it is in fact a challenge to

---

[1] Prime minister of Israel from 1948 to 1963.

[2] David Ben-Gurion, *Rebirth and Destiny of Israel* (New York: Philosophical Library, 1954), 489.

[3] The Conference of the Heads of African States held in Casablanca, Morocco, in January 1961.

[4] The First Conference of the Heads of State or Government of Non-Aligned Countries took place in Belgrade, Yugoslavia (now Serbia), in September 1961.

all anti-colonial peoples in Asia and Africa. For, in the final analysis, the cause of anti-colonialism and liberation is one and indivisible.

And—as a racist system animated by doctrines of racial self-segregation, racial exclusiveness, and racial supremacy, and methodically translating these doctrines into ruthless practices of racial discrimination and oppression—the political systems erected by Zionist colonists in Palestine cannot fail to be recognized as a menace by all *civilized men* dedicated to the safeguarding and enhancement of the dignity of man. For whenever and wherever the dignity of but one single human being is violated, in pursuance of the creed of racism, a heinous sin is committed against the dignity of all men, everywhere.

38

CLAUDIA JONES

The Caribbean Community in Britain

1964

The era of decolonization also saw the emergence of massive emigration from some of the very areas of the world that were becoming independent to Western Europe. Often, these non-Europeans settled in the metropoles that had colonized their homeland, whether the large numbers of Algerians who moved to France or, as revealed in this excerpt, the West Indians who settled in Great Britain. During the 1960s and 1970s, such movements of people sparked many discussions about what decolonization meant. They also emphasized that the connections between lands and peoples that imperialism had created and that colonialism had deepened would not simply disappear when political independence occurred.

Claudia Jones was one of the first to analyze what large-scale emigration from former colonies to the metropoles meant from a left-wing perspective. Jones was born in Trinidad, but her family immigrated to the United States when she was nine. Too poor to attend college, she worked in various menial jobs. In 1936, she joined the Communist Party of the United States (CPUSA), and she quickly took on important roles both at

From *Freedomways* 4 (Summer 1964): 341–44, 353.

various publications linked to the party and within Communist organizations. Much of her work sought to integrate analyses of racism into the CPUSA's focus on economic concerns and class identities, as she made clear in her most well-known publication, An End to the Neglect of the Problems of the Negro Woman! *(1949).*

Between 1948 and 1955, her membership in the CPUSA resulted in four prison terms, after which she was expelled from the United States and found refuge in the United Kingdom. Though still a committed Communist, she did not join the British Communist party, which she saw as uninterested in the questions that most interested her: antiracism and anti-imperialism. This journal article was her final publication. She died in 1964 at the age of forty-nine.

Over a quarter of a million West Indians, the overwhelming majority of them from Jamaica, have now settled in Britain in less than a decade. Britain has become, in the mid-1960's, the center of the largest overseas population of West Indians; numerically relegating to second place, the once superior community of West Indians in the United States.

This new situation in Britain, has been inimitably described in the discerning verse of Louise Bennett, noted Jamaican folklorist, as "Colonization in Reverse."[1] . . .

Emigration from the West Indies has served for over two generations as a palliative, a stop-gap measure to ease the growing economic frustrations in a largely impoverished agricultural economy; in which under colonial-capitalist-imperialist relations, the wealth of these islands is dominated by the few, with the vast majority of the people living under unbearable conditions.

It was the outstanding Cuban poet, Nicholas Guillen [*sic*], who noting a situation (also observed by other West Indian writers) in which the young generation, most of it out of work, "chafing at the bit," seeing as their only hope a swift opportunity to leave their islands, lamented thus: *"Scant, sea-girt land, Oh, tight squeezed land. . . ."*

Indeed, as with all migrant populations here is mirrored in extension the existing problems of the nations and territories from which the

---

[1] Bennett's poem "Colonization in Reverse," to which Jones refers, was published in 1966. Written in Jamaican patois (the local dialect), its first stanza reads: "What a joyful news, Miss Mattie; / Ah feel like me heart gwine burs / Jamaica people colonizin / Englan in reverse." (Louise Bennett, "Colonization in Reverse," in *The Penguin Book of Caribbean Verse in English*, ed. Paula Burnett [Harmondsworth, U.K.: Penguin Books, 1986], 32–33.)

migrants originally spring. West Indian emigration to the United Kingdom is no exception to this phenomenon. Furthermore, this emigration, as with many other Afro-Asian peoples, has occurred almost immediately prior to the achievement of political independence in two of the largest of the West Indies islands [Jamaica and Trinidad and Tobago became independent in 1962]. *It is because prospects have not yet qualitatively improved for the vast majority of the West Indian workers and people, inhibited by the tenaciousness of continued Anglo-American imperialist dominance over West Indian economic life, that this emigratory movement of people from the West Indies continues.* History will undoubtedly evaluate this development as, in part, attributable to the demise of the West Indian Federation[2] and the consequent smashing of wide hopes for the establishment of a united West Indian nation in which freedom of movement would have absorbed some of our disinherited, disillusioned, and unfulfilled people who were compelled to leave their homelands in order to survive.

. . . Another influence, was that post-war Britain, experiencing a brief economic boom, and full employment, needed overseas and cheap labor to staff the semi-skilled and non-skilled vacancies, the results of temporary postwar economic incline. Britain sought West Indian immigration as an indispensable aid to the British economy; indeed, encouraged it!

The presence of West Indian immigrants (who together with other Afro-Asian peoples total nearly a half million people) represent less than one per cent in an overall Anglo-populous of 52 million. But even this small minority has given rise to a plethora of new sociological and analytical works such as *"Newcomers"; "Colored Immigrants in Britain"; "The Economic and Social Position of Negro Immigrants in Britain"; "Black and White in Harmony"; "Colored Minorities in Britain"; "Colonial Students"; "Report on West Indian Accommodation Problems in the United Kingdom"; "Race and Racism"; "Dark Strangers"; "They Seek a Living."*

Extreme manifestations of the racialism which underlies the present status of West Indians in Britain were graphically witnessed in late 1958, when racial riots occurred in Notting Hill and Nottingham. These events, which followed the as yet unsolved murder of a St. Vincentian, Mr. Kelso Cochrane, claimed world headlines. Clashes even occurred between West Indian and other Afro-Asian migrants with white Britons. The firm handling of the provocateurs by the authorities, following the wide protests of immigrants, labor, Communist and progressive

2 See the headnote to Document 27.

forces, and the intervention of the West Indian Federal leaders, for a time quelled the overt racialists, and the "keep Britain white, fascist-propagandists." But the canker of racialism was now nakedly revealed. It exposed also the smugness of official Britain, who hitherto pointed to racial manifestations in Little Rock [Arkansas] and Johannesburg, South Africa, but continued to deny its existence in Britain.

Today, new problems, underscored by the Tory [Conservative party] Government's enactment, and recent renewal of the 1962 Commonwealth Immigration Act (one which ostensibly restricts Commonwealth immigration as a whole, but in fact, discriminates heavily against colored Commonwealth citizens) has established a second-class citizenship status for West Indians and other Afro-Asian peoples in Britain. Accompanying the general social problems confronting all new migrant workers, West Indians, stemming as they do in large measure from African origins, are experiencing sharper color-bar practices. In common with other workers, the West Indians take part in the struggle for defense and improvement of their working and living standards. But the growing intensity of racialism forces them, as it does other Afro-Asians, to join and found their own organizations. In fact, their status is more and more a barometer of British intentions and claims of a so-called "Multi-racial Commonwealth." As put in one of the recent sociological studies of a West Indian migrant group in Brixton, financed by the Institute of Race Relations and the Nuffield Foundation:

> Now that the whole equilibrium of world power is changing, and the Commonwealth is, by virtue of conscious British policy being transformed from a family based on kinship, to a wider multi-racial *familia*, the presence of colored immigrants in Britain, presents a moral and a practical challenge. The people of these islands face the need not only to reformulate their views of Britain's role and status in such a Commonwealth, but also to apply the new relationships in their dealings with colored Commonwealth migrants here at home. And not only the color-conscious migrants themselves, but the newly-independent Afro-Asian countries and the outside world as a whole, show an inclination to judge Britain's good faith in international relations by her ability to put her own house in order.

> from *Dark Strangers* [*: A Sociological Study of the Absorption of a Recent West Indian Migrant Group in Brixton*, 1963], by Sheila Patterson

. . . Conscious therefore of the need for alleviation of their second-class citizenship, determined to live and work in human dignity as is their natural right, the resourceful West Indian migrant[s], in common with all peoples involved (either consciously or not) in anti-imperialist struggles, are also thinking about their ultimate direction. That they are only now at the stage of tentatively formulating their views may be ascribed to three main factors: 1) to the constant pressure and concern with daily problems of survival, 2) to the groping in their own minds for the fundamental significance of their national identity, and 3) to the lack of an organized perspective for a progressive, united West Indies at home.

39

KWAME NKRUMAH

Neo-Colonialism: The Last Stage of Imperialism

1965

During the 1950s, Kwame Nkrumah described the nonviolent approach he and his party took to win independence in Ghana in 1957 as "positive action," which he defined as "seeking social justice" through "the destruction of oligarchic exploitation and oppression."[3] *In the multiple books he published following independence, Nkrumah developed the concepts that he thought crucial to the creation of social justice. He argued that there were important conflicts between different groups, which were caused by contradictory interests. This attention to conflict draws from Marxism. Yet unlike Marxist claims that conflicts of interests are best explained in terms of social classes, Nkrumah saw conflicts between certain types of nations as more important. This, he argued, was because imperialism had altered capitalism and forged new bonds between people whom Marxists claimed were in conflict. The most important current conflict, in his view, was between the developing world and the developed world (which he defined as Europe's former colonial powers and the United States). In his view, the developed world would view the positive actions of developing countries as a threat and act to limit their impact. He argued that*

[3] Kwame Nkrumah, *Consciencism. Philosophy and Ideology for Decolonization* (New York: Monthly Review Press, 1970), 99.

From Kwame Nkrumah, *Neo-Colonialism: The Last Stage of Imperialism* (New York: International Publishers, 1965), ix–xiii.

popular mobilization could offer the developing world—and Africa especially—the ability to overcome the economic and military advantages of the developed world. To fully benefit from popular mobilization, Nkrumah argued, "Africa must unite" (the title of one of his books). It was necessary, in his view, for newly independent nation-states to join together into one large unit.

By the early 1960s, Nkrumah's role in Ghana and his writings had made him one of the most influential analysts of contemporary Africa. It was in these same years that his efforts to educate and modernize Ghana and to establish political unity among all of Africa's independent states came to seem doomed to failure. The price of Ghana's most important export, cocoa, plunged. The International Monetary Fund (IMF) put intense pressure on Nkrumah's government to change its policies. The few institutional links between African states collapsed, and no others emerged.

The following excerpt is from a book in which Nkrumah analyzed this situation, which he argued resulted from what he called "neo-colonialism." Many outside observers thought that the book, Neo-Colonialism: The Last Stage of Imperialism, *marked a radicalization of Nkrumah's argument. Several years later, he moved away from positive action, calling instead for an African Socialist Revolution. This was after he had been removed from power in a 1966 coup d'état staged by members of the Ghanaian armed forces.*

The neo-colonialism of today represents imperialism in its final and perhaps its most dangerous stage. In the past it was possible to convert a country upon which a neo-colonial regime had been imposed—Egypt in the nineteenth century is an example—into a colonial territory. Today this process is no longer feasible. Old-fashioned colonialism is by no means entirely abolished. It still constitutes an African problem, but it is everywhere on the retreat. Once a territory has become nominally independent it is no longer possible, as it was in the last century, to reverse the process. Existing colonies may linger on, but no new colonies will be created. In place of colonialism as the main instrument of imperialism we have today neo-colonialism.

The essence of neo-colonialism is that the State which is subject to it is, in theory, independent and has all the outward trappings of international sovereignty. In reality its economic system and thus its political policy is directed from outside.

The methods and form of this direction can take various shapes. For example, in an extreme case the troops of the imperial power may garrison the territory of the neo-colonial State and control the government of it. More often, however, neo-colonialist control is exercised through economic or monetary means. The neo-colonial State may be obliged to take the manufactured products of the imperialist power to the exclusion of competing products from elsewhere. Control over government policy in the neo-colonial State may be secured by payments towards the cost of running the State, by the provision of civil servants in positions where they can dictate policy, and by monetary control over foreign exchange through the imposition of a banking system controlled by the imperial power.

Where neo-colonialism exists the power exercising control is often the State which formerly ruled the territory in question, but this is not necessarily so. For example, in the case of South Vietnam the former imperial power was France, but neo-colonial control of the State has now gone to the United States. . . .

The result of neo-colonialism is that foreign capital is used for the exploitation rather than for the development of the less developed parts of the world. Investment under neo-colonialism increases rather than decreases the gap between the rich and the poor countries of the world.

The struggle against neo-colonialism is not aimed at excluding the capital of the developed world from operating in less developed countries. It is aimed at preventing the financial power of the developed countries being used in such a way as to impoverish the less developed.

. . . The question is one of power. A State in the grip of neo-colonialism is not master of its own destiny. It is this factor which makes neo-colonialism such a serious threat to world peace. The growth of nuclear weapons has made out of date the old-fashioned balance of power which rested upon the ultimate sanction of a major war. Certainty of mutual mass destruction effectively prevents either of the great power blocs from threatening the other with the possibility of a world-wide war, and military conflict has thus become confined to "limited wars." For these neo-colonialism is the breeding ground. . . .

Neo-colonialism is also the worst form of imperialism. For those who practise it, it means power without responsibility and for those who suffer from it, it means exploitation without redress. In the days of old-fashioned colonialism, the imperial power had at least to explain and justify at home the actions it was taking abroad. In the colony those who served the ruling imperial power could at least look to its protection against any violent move by their opponents. With neo-colonialism neither is the case.

Above all, neo-colonialism, like colonialism before it, postpones the facing of the social issues which will have to be faced by the fully developed sector of the world before the danger of world war can be eliminated or the problem of world poverty resolved.

Neo-colonialism, like colonialism, is an attempt to export the social conflicts of the capitalist countries. The temporary success of this policy can be seen in the ever-widening gap between the richer and the poorer nations of the world. But the internal contradictions and conflicts of neo-colonialism make it certain that it cannot endure as a permanent world policy. How it should be brought to an end is a problem that should be studied, above all, by the developed nations of the world, because it is they who will feel the full impact of the ultimate failure. The longer it continues the more certain it is that its inevitable collapse will destroy the social system of which they have made it a foundation. . . .

The post-war period inaugurated a very different colonial policy. A deliberate attempt was made to divert colonial earnings from the wealthy class and use them instead generally to finance the "Welfare State." . . . This was the method consciously adopted even by those working-class leaders who had before the war regarded the colonial peoples as their natural allies against their capitalist enemies at home.

At first it was presumed that this object could be achieved by maintaining the prewar colonial system. Experience soon proved that attempts to do so would be disastrous and would only provoke colonial wars, thus dissipating the anticipated gains from the continuance of the colonial regime. Britain, in particular, realised this at an early stage and the correctness of the British judgement at the time has subsequently been demonstrated by the defeat of French colonialism in the Far East and Algeria and the failure of the Dutch to retain any of their former colonial empire.

The system of neo-colonialism was therefore instituted and in the short run it has served the developed powers admirably. It is in the long run that its consequences are likely to be catastrophic for them.

A Chronology of the Era of Decolonization (1937–1965)

**1937–
1945** World War II.

1941 *August* U.S. president Franklin Roosevelt and British prime minister Winston Churchill sign Atlantic Charter.

1942 "Quit India" movements begin.

1945 *May* "Victory in Europe" sparks violent protests against colonial rule in Damascus (Syria), eastern Algeria, and elsewhere; European governments respond with harsh reprisals.

August "Victory in Japan" leads to end of Japanese colonial rule in Korea and Manchuria, which returns, with Taiwan, to Chinese rule in October.

September 2 Ho Chi Minh announces Vietnamese independence; French troops move to reassert control.

1946 United States recognizes Philippine independence; constitution of Fourth Republic declares that French empire is now French Union.

1947 India and Pakistan gain independence from British rule.

1948 Burma and Ceylon (present-day Sri Lanka) gain independence from Britain; United Nations dissolves British mandate of Palestine, which leads to Israeli independence; Republic of Korea (South) and Democratic People's Republic of Korea (North) gain independence; Union of South Africa votes first laws that will become part of apartheid system.

1949 People's Republic of China established; Indonesia (formerly Dutch East Indies) obtains independence.

1950 USSR and its allies recognize Democratic Republic of Vietnam; United States and some of its allies recognize government of

Bao Dai, head of State of Vietnam, which remains part of French Union; UNESCO publishes "The Statement on Race."

1951 Libya gains independence from Italy.

1952 Military coup d'état leads to overthrow of Egypt's King Farouk and establishment of a military council headed by Gamal Abdel Nasser, which moves to end British occupation; Britain declares state of emergency to crush Land and Freedom Army (LFA) movement (which British called Mau Mau) in Kenya.

1953 Cambodia and Laos gain formal independence from France; Soviet leader Joseph Stalin dies.

1954 *May* French troops defeated by (North) Vietnamese troops at Dien Bien Phu.

July Geneva Agreements separate Vietnam into two zones, a northern Communist zone and a southern non-Communist zone, and lead to independence for State of Vietnam (South Vietnam).

November 1 National Liberation Front (FLN) launches attacks across Algeria in support of independence.

1955 *April* Afro-Asian Conference held in Bandung, Indonesia; National Organization of Cypriot Combatants (EOKA) begins campaign of violent attacks on civilians and British forces to end British rule and unite with Greece.

1956 Suez Crisis over Egypt's nationalization of Suez Canal; Sudan gains independence from Britain and Egypt; Tunisia and Morocco win independence from France.

1957 Gold Coast gains independence from Britain as Ghana, under leadership of Kwame Nkrumah; Malaya becomes independent from Britain.

1958 Conference of Independent African States (April) and All African People's conference (December), both in Accra, Ghana; Guinea becomes independent from France; Syria and Egypt become United Arab Republic (UAR); British declare end of anti–"Mau Mau" state of emergency in Kenya.

1959 Cuban revolutionaries overthrow U.S.-supported government.

1960 Somalia gains independence from Italy and Britain; Cameroon becomes independent from Britain and France; Senegal, Mali, Dahomey (becomes Benin in 1975), Niger, Burkina Faso, Mauritania, Togo (previously French Togoland), Côte d'Ivoire, Chad, Central African Republic (previously Ubangi-Shari), Congo-Brazzaville, Gabon, and Madagascar (previously Malagasy Protectorate) gain independence from France; Belgian Congo gains independence from Belgium as Democratic Republic of the

Congo; Nigeria becomes independent from Britain; split between USSR and People's Republic of China becomes public; British prime minister Harold Macmillan gives "Wind of Change" speech before South Africa's parliament.

1961 Sierra Leone, Tanganyika, and Kuwait gain independence from Britain; South Africa leaves British Commonwealth, becomes Republic of South Africa; armed struggle for Angola's independence begins; first U.S. personnel arrive in (South) Vietnam; Syria secedes from UAR; Frantz Fanon dies shortly after publication of his last book, *The Wretched of the Earth*.

1962 Algeria becomes independent from France; Jamaica, Trinidad and Tobago, and Uganda gain independence from Britain; Ruanda-Urundi leaves Belgian control to become Rwanda and Burundi; Cuban missile crisis.

1963 British East Africa becomes Kenya and Uganda; Zanzibar gains independence from Britain; Organization of African Unity formed.

1964 Nyasaland becomes Malawi, and Northern Rhodesia becomes Zambia (both gaining independence from Britain); Samoa gains independence from New Zealand; Nelson Mandela, leader of African National Congress (South Africa), condemned to life in prison; former British colonies Zanzibar and Tanganyika unite to form Tanzania; Palestine Liberation Organization founded; armed struggle for an independent Mozambique begins.

1965 Gambia and Maldives obtain independence from Britain; Southern Rhodesia declares independence from Britain under white-minority rule; Japan and Republic of Korea (South Korea) establish diplomatic relations; U.S.-supported military coup ousts Indonesian leader Sukarno; Fatah begins armed attacks on Israeli targets.

Questions for Consideration

1. Why did the era of decolonization happen when it did? Was it inevitable?

2. What were some of the effects of World War II on the emergence of decolonization as an international phenomenon? See especially Documents 1–3 and 6.

3. Why were so many European leaders reluctant to allow their colonies to gain independence? See especially Documents 1, 20, 24, 27, and 33.

4. What positions did the United States take in international debates about decolonization? What factors complicated the choices available to U.S. officials? What roles did decolonization play in U.S. domestic political debates, including the civil rights movement? See especially Documents 1, 4, 9, and 38.

5. How did colonial and anticolonial actors appeal to international public opinion in order to advance their projects? What types of arguments did they make, and by what means did they disseminate their arguments? How important were such efforts in affecting events on the ground? See especially Documents 3, 4, 8, 9, 12–14, 19, 20, 23–25, 31, 32, 34, 35, 37, and 39.

6. In what ways did the new importance of international institutions and forums (e.g., the United Nations and UNESCO) influence how colonizers and anticolonial activists defined their decisions or took action? What effects, if any, did the growing importance of anticolonialism have on the development of international institutions and forums? See especially Documents 2, 5, 6, 8, 9, 16, 19, 32, 34, and 35.

7. How did critiques of racism become so linked to critiques of European colonialism? Was it possible to make arguments that were at once antiracist and in favor of maintaining existing connections between metropoles and colonies? See especially Documents 5–10, 20, 22–30, 32, and 37–39.

8. How did questions of morality and ethics shape arguments for and against the continuation of colonial rule? How did religious arguments

influence moral and ethical debates? See especially Documents 4, 9–11, 16, 18, 22, 26–29, 31, and 33.

9. In what ways did women participate in the decolonization movements? How did *women* and *family* provide useful metaphors that allowed both colonialists and anticolonialists to advance their arguments? See especially Documents 11–13, 31, 34, and 38.

10. What were some of the ways that Communist ideology influenced anticolonial actors? What were some of the ways that anticommunism influenced those who fought for continued European rule? See especially Documents 3, 5, 7–9, 15, 23, 24–26, 33, 34, 38, and 39.

11. How did the cold war shape the history of decolonization? How did the growing importance of anticolonialism affect the cold war? See especially Documents 7–9, 23, 30, 32–35, 36, and 38.

12. What were some of the interpretations different people gave to the concept of the third world? Were all of them consistent with Alfred Sauvy's original definition? Why was the idea of the third world so widely discussed? See especially Documents 7–9, 14, 24, 30, 32, and 35.

13. How did various actors, whether supportive or critical of continued European rule, describe the historical moment they were living in? How did they see their own historical context as influencing the choices available to them? What leaders most effectively interpreted the past to advance their goals?

14. Why did violence become an increasingly important factor in struggles over decolonization? What justifications explained the use of violence? How, why, and by whom was the accusation "terrorism" used? See especially Documents 11–13, 16, 17, 19, 20, 23, 25, 26, 31, 34, 35, and 36.

15. Why did so many contemporary observers describe the violence of anticolonial rebels as different in kind from violence used to defend colonial regimes? What, if anything, distinguished the violence employed on both sides? See especially Documents 12, 13, 16, 17, 19, 20, 22–23, 25, 26, 31, 34, 35, and 36.

16. How did French officials explain why they needed to remain in Algeria? Whom were they trying to convince? What arguments did they use to target different groups of people? How did their arguments change over time? See especially Documents 20 and 23.

17. On what bases did the National Liberation Front (FLN) claim to represent all Algerians? What arguments did others make that rejected the FLN's claim? In this respect, was the FLN typical of or different from other anticolonial movements? See especially Documents 3, 10, 14, 16, 19, 20, 23, 25, 28, and 29.

18. How did Frantz Fanon link the evidence he drew from the Algerian struggle to larger claims about the colonial situation? See Document 25.

19. What role did economics play in arguments for and against decolonization? See especially Documents 5, 7, 18, 21, 24, 27, 28, 29, 34, 37, and 38.

20. Many of the documents collected here are official government documents, while others are not. Why is it particularly important to include both types of documents when seeking to understand the history of decolonization?

Selected Bibliography

GENERAL WORKS

Betts, Raymond F. *Decolonization*. New York: Routledge, 1998.

Birmingham, David. *The Decolonization of Africa*. Athens: Ohio University Press, 1996.

Gifford, Prosser, and William Roger Louis, eds. *Decolonization and African Independence: The Transfers of Power, 1960–1980*. New Haven, Conn.: Yale University Press, 1988.

———. *The Transfer of Power in Africa: Decolonization, 1940–1960*. New Haven, Conn.: Yale University Press, 1982.

Heinlein, Frank. *British Government Policy and Decolonisation, 1945–1963: Scrutinising the Official Mind*. New York: Routledge, 2002.

Holland, R. F. *European Decolonization, 1918–81*. Basingstoke, U.K.: Palgrave Macmillan, 1985.

Le Sueur, James D. *The Decolonization Reader*. New York: Routledge, 2003.

Shipway, Martin. *Decolonization and Its Impact: A Comparative Approach to the End of the Colonial Empires*. Oxford, U.K.: Blackwell, 2008.

1945–1947: DECOLONIZATION BECOMES IMAGINABLE

Aydin, Cemil. *Politics of Anti-Westernism in Asia: Visions of World Order in Pan-Islamic and Pan-Asian Thought*. New York: Columbia University Press, 2007.

Chatterjee, Partha. *The Nation and Its Fragments: Colonial and Postcolonial Histories*. Princeton, N.J.: Princeton University Press, 1993.

Cooper, Frederick. *Africa since 1940: The Past of the Present*. Cambridge, U.K.: Cambridge University Press, 2002.

———. *Decolonization and African Society: The Labor Question in French and British Africa*. Cambridge, U.K.: Cambridge University Press, 1996.

Darwin, John. *Britain and Decolonization: Retreat from Empire in the Postwar World*. Basingstoke, U.K.: Palgrave Macmillan, 1988.

Derrick, Jonathan. *Africa's "Agitators": Militant Anti-colonialism in Africa and the West, 1918–1939*. London: Hurst, 2008.

Kent, John. *The Internationalization of Colonialism: Britain, France, and Black Africa, 1939–1956*. Oxford, U.K.: Clarendon Press, 1992.

Logevall, Fredrik. *Embers of War: The Fall of an Empire and the Making of America's Vietnam*. New York: Random House, 2012.

Low, D. A. *Eclipse of Empire*. Cambridge, U.K.: Cambridge University Press, 1993.

DEFINING NEW INTERNATIONAL CONNECTIONS

Connelly, Matthew. *A Diplomatic Revolution: Algeria's Fight for Independence and the Origins of the Post–Cold War Era*. New York: Oxford University Press, 2002.

Fedorowich, Kent, and Martin Thomas, eds. *International Diplomacy and Colonial Retreat*. London: Frank Cass, 2001.

Kanet, Roger. "The Superpower Quest for Empire: The Cold War and Soviet Support for 'Wars of National Liberation.'" *Cold War History* 6, no. 3 (2006): 331–52.

Lee, Christopher, ed. *Making a World after Empire: The Bandung Moment and Its Political Afterlives*. Athens: Ohio University Press, 2010.

Mazower, Mark. *No Enchanted Palace: The End of Empire and the Ideological Origins of the United Nations*. Princeton, N.J.: Princeton University Press, 2009.

Westad, Odd Arne. *The Global Cold War: Third World Interventions and the Making of Our Times*. Cambridge, U.K.: Cambridge University Press, 2005.

Zubok, Vladislav, and Constantine Pleshakov. *Inside the Kremlin's Cold War: From Stalin to Khrushchev*. Cambridge, Mass.: Harvard University Press, 1996.

FROM POSSIBILITIES OF INDEPENDENCE TO EXPECTATIONS OF LIBERATION

Anderson, David. *Histories of the Hanged: Britain's Dirty War in Kenya and the End of Empire*. London: Weidenfeld & Nicolson, 2005.

Birmingham, David. *Kwame Nkrumah: The Father of African Nationalism*. Athens: Ohio University Press, 1998.

Borstelmann, Thomas. *The Cold War and the Color Line: American Race Relations in the Global Arena*. Cambridge, Mass.: Harvard University Press, 2002.

Fieldhouse, David Kenneth. *Black Africa, 1945–1980: Economic Decolonization and Arrested Development*. London: Routledge, 2012.

Klose, Fabian. *Human Rights in the Shadow of Colonial Violence: The Wars of Independence in Kenya and Algeria*. Philadelphia: University of Pennsylvania Press, 2013.

Odhiambo, E. S. Atieno, and John Lonsdale, eds. *Mau Mau & Nationhood: Arms, Authority & Narration*. Oxford, U.K.: James Currey, 2002.

THE TRIUMPH OF ANTICOLONIALISM

Evans, Martin. *Algeria: France's Undeclared War*. New York: Oxford University Press, 2012.

Horne, Alistair. *A Savage War of Peace: Algeria, 1954–1962*. New York: New York Review of Books Classics, 2006.

Mawby, Spencer. *Ordering Independence: The End of Empire in the Anglophone Caribbean, 1947–69*. Basingstoke, U.K.: Palgrave Macmillan, 2012.

Shepard, Todd. *The Invention of Decolonization: The Algerian War and the Remaking of France*, 2nd ed. Ithaca, N.Y.: Cornell University Press, 2008.

THE CONTAGION OF INDEPENDENCE

Mamdani, Mahmood. *Citizen and Subject: Contemporary Africa and the Legacy of Late Colonialism*. Princeton, N.J.: Princeton University Press, 1996.

Paul, Kathleen. *Whitewashing Britain: Race and Citizenship in the Postwar Era*. Ithaca, N.Y.: Cornell University Press, 1997.

Posel, Deborah. *The Making of Apartheid, 1948–1961: Conflict and Compromise*. Oxford, U.K.: Clarendon Press, 1991.

Robinson, Shira. *Citizen Strangers: Palestinians and the Birth of Israel's Liberal Settler State*. Palo Alto, Calif.: Stanford University Press, 2013.

Seton-Hall, Hugh, ed. "Imperial Hangovers." Special issue, *Journal of Contemporary History* 15, no. 1 (January 1980).

Acknowledgments (*continued from p. iv*)

Document 6. "Statement by Experts on Race Problems," July 20, 1950, © UNESCO, 1950. Used by permission of UNESCO.

Document 7. From "Trois mondes, une planète," by Alfred Sauvy, *L'Observateur* 118 (August 14, 1952), 14. Used by permission of *Le Nouvel Observateur*. Translation by Todd Shepard.

Document 9. From "The Color Curtain" by Richard Wright. Copyright © 1956 Richard Wright. Reprinted by permission of John Hawkins & Associates, Inc., and the Estate of Richard Wright.

Document 10. "Song of Africa" from *Mau Mau Detainee*, by Josiah Mwangi Kariuki (Oxford: Oxford University Press, 1963). Used by permission of Doris Nyambura Mwangi.

Document 15. From Israel State Archives, Jerusalem: File 102/GL17013/9. Original document used by permission of Israel State Archives. Translation by Shira Robinson with assistance from Yonay Israel.

Document 18. From *L'incendie* by Mohammed Dib. © 1956 Éditions du Seuil, 1989. Reprinted by permission of Éditions du Seuil.

Document 21. "Locust, Leave My Country," by Slimane Azem from Chants kabyles de la guerre d'indépendence: Algérie 1954–1962 (*Kabyle Songs of the War for Independence: Algeria 1954–1962*), edited by Mehenna Mahfoufi (Paris: Seguier, 2002). Used by permission of Mehenna Mahfoufi.

Document 25. Excerpts from *The Wretched of the Earth*, by Frantz Fanon, copyright © 1963 by Présence Africaine. Used by permission of Grove/Atlantic, Inc. Any third party use of this material, outside of this publication, is prohibited.

Document 31. "The Child Who Was Shot Dead by Soldiers at Nyanga," by Ingrid Jonker, translated by Jack Cope; in Ann Harries, Roger Diski, and Alasdair Brown, *The Child Is Not Dead: Youth Resistance in South Africa, 1976–86* (London: British Defence and Aid Fund for Southern Africa, 1986), 12. Copyright The Ingrid Jonker Trust. Used by permission.

Document 32. From "Declaration on the Granting of Independence to Colonial Countries and Peoples," UN General Assembly, 14 December 1960, A/RES/1514, © 1960 United Nations. Reprinted with the permission of the United Nations.

Document 33. "Ten Principles" translation by Gabriel Paquette based on the original document kindly made available by Dr. Luis B. Serapião from his personal papers.

Document 35. "Anonymous Soldiers for the United Nations" from *Revolution in Guinea, Stage 1* by Amilcar Cabral, London, 1974. Used by permission of Monthly Review Foundation.

Document 36. "Record of Conversation between Soviet Ambassador to China S. V. Chervonenko and Chinese Prime Minister Zhou Enlai on 13 April 1965 (excerpt) from "History and Public Policy Program Digital Archive, AVPRF, opis 0100, fond 58, papka 516, delo 5, listy 101–27. Obtained and translated by Sergey Radchenko. http://digital archive.wilsoncenter.org/document/112454. Used by permission of the Woodrow Wilson International Center for Scholars.

Document 39. From *Neo-Colonialism: The Last Stage of Imperialism*, by Kwame Nkrumah (New York: International Publishers, 1965). Used by permission of International Publications/N.Y.

Index